GIRLS AND BOYS IN SCHOOL

Together or Separate?

GIRLS AND BOYS IN SCHOOL
Together or Separate?

Cornelius Riordan

Foreword by James S. Coleman

TEACHERS COLLEGE, COLUMBIA UNIVERSITY
New York and London

Published by Teachers College Press, 1234 Amsterdam Avenue
New York, NY 10027

Library of Congress Cataloging-in-Publication Data

Riordan, Cornelius H., 1940–
    Girls and boys in school : together or separate? / Cornelius
Riordan.
        p.   cm.
    Includes bibliographical references.
    ISBN 0-8077-2993-0 (alk. paper). — ISBN 0-8077-2992-2 (pbk. :
alk. paper)
        1. Coeducation—United States.   2. Education—United States—
History   3. Sex differences in education—United States.
I. Title.
LB3066.R56   1990
372—dc20   89-38053
                                                                    CIP

ISBN 0-8077-2922-2 (pbk.)
     0-8077-2993-0

Printed on acid-free paper
Manufactured in the United States of America

97 96 95 94 93 92 91 90   8 7 6 5 4 3 2 1

To
Kate and Julie

Contents

Foreword

In many areas of society, institutional arrangements follow a conventional wisdom, undisturbed by research. A major role of applied social research is to test these institutional arrangements, and to confirm the conventional wisdom or to expose it as incorrect. Yet it is often true that the conventional wisdom is strong enough to inhibit research into the area in question. If there is a societal consensus that one institution is *right*, then even the researcher may act as a self-censoring agent, steering away from research that questions this rightness.

Coeducation is such an institution. Like other institutions held in place by conventional wisdom, coeducation is held to be right, in part because of its contribution to other, more strongly held values. One of these values in the case of coeducation is that of educational equality for men and women. The presumption is that educational equality is furthered by coeducation, that single-sex education is inherently unequal.

It is easy to see how this presumption gained currency. Single-sex schooling was, at the outset, schooling for boys. Schooling for girls was an afterthought, either in single-sex institutions of their own, or with boys, where small numbers made single-sex institutions inefficient. Boys' schools, however, were dominant, and the elimination of single-sex schooling could be seen as elimination of that dominance.

A second way that conventional wisdom about institutional arrangements comes into being is through the discarding of values on which a set of institutions was based, as a new value consensus replaces the earlier one. Single-sex schools were in part based on a set of values about what was the proper degree and kind of contact between boys and girls after puberty. These values, now labeled "Victorian," have long since been replaced by others, as precepts based on psychology have replaced those with religious roots. This replacement of values occurred through a social conflict, and single-sex schools were on the losing side of that conflict. The interests of the winning side in eliminating all the institutions connected with Victorian values added force to the elimination of single-sex schools.

Yet this leaves unanswered certain questions of fact: Just what are the consequences of single-sex and coeducational schools for those who pass through them? Specifically, what are the intellectual consequences, the psychological consequences, and the social consequences? How do achievement levels compare, how does college attendance compare, how do career paths compare, and how do marriages and divorces compare? One would have thought that such a question would be an obvious one, certain to engage the attention of sociologists of education. But the force of conventional values affects even their research, so that without anyone intending it, the topic has remained largely ignored.

In such circumstances, there may come along a few researchers who, for whatever reason, are sufficiently unafflicted by the value consensus to raise the avoided question. Cornelius Riordan has done this, in his book. He has not examined all the relevant consequences (though he has examined many, both short- and long-term) and he has not provided uncontestable answers to those he has examined. But he has done the important task: He has helped to throw open the question that had been by premature presumption closed. He examines achievement growth and a variety of long-term occupational, psychological, and social outcomes for men and women who attended coeducational and single-sex schools.

The results of these analyses are not simple and straightforward. They differ for males and females. The difference raises the questions once more: Did the elimination of single-sex schools reduce male dominance, as implicitly assumed, or did it instead bring about a new dominance within schools? Do the social processes within schools have a greater impact on educational outcomes than do invidious comparisons between schools?

Riordan's analyses cannot answer these questions. However, what his work does is to initiate the painstaking task of first discovering the effects of these institutional arrangements on outcomes, and then discovering the social processes through which these effects occur.

JAMES S. COLEMAN
THE UNIVERSITY OF CHICAGO

Preface

Some people will challenge the views presented in this book. They will argue that single-sex education is an overly risky step backwards. Women were first excluded altogether from schools, and then only a century or two ago, allowed to have schools of their own. These separate schools for girls, some will contend, were inferior in almost every way to boys' schools, and only coeducation can provide equal educational opportunity. Hence, proposals for single-sex schools or classrooms seem to be a step in reverse.

I appreciate these concerns. They are extremely important and not without some basis. But they are not foolproof either. The education of girls and women may have benefited in the short run from the expansion of mixed-sex schools. Undoubtedly, at the lower levels of education, the commitment to equality and universality has made it possible for women to reduce much of the existing male/female gap in educational attainment. Yet, as I document in this book, many problems remain, and some appear to be intractable.

Some people feel that all-girls schools, as they developed historically, were inferior to all-boys schools or to mixed-sex institutions. Is there any evidence for this? I don't think that anyone knows for sure. Historically, boys had better facilities and they still do. But if there is one single thing that we have learned about effective schools over the past 30 years, it is that the physical resources of a school have little influence on the quality or quantity of education that ensue from the facility. I think that any close-order examination of facilities in modern-day mixed-sex schools will show that boys still get to use and/or spend the most expensive resources, such as electronic and science equipment, football equipment, and other athletic support.

My own view, based on the logic developed throughout the book, is that girls' schools have been superior to boys' schools from the very beginning, because of an academic-value climate as opposed to the adolescent-value climate that was assuredly more dominant in the boys' schools. By the same logic, I think that all-girls schools can be considered superior to early coeducational schools in terms of academic outcomes, especially when girls are compared to girls. Contrary to popular opinion, I believe that all-girls schools consistently have provided a more effective educational environment *for girls* than have mixed-sex schools.

But what if I am wrong about the above argument? I think there is still ample justification for exploring single-sex schools in the *limited* form that I have advised. Anyone who spends 30 minutes in a typical high school anywhere, or talks for 30 minutes with a high school student over matters other than sports, cars, soap operas, rock concerts, dating, and designer clothes knows two things: (1) that our schools are in serious trouble, and (2) that no words or commission reports or studies such as this can convey just how bad the situation is. We try to describe what is going on in school with words like *disengagement, alienation, mediocrity,* and *accommodation.* But these words simply do not carry the burden of describing the depth or dimensions of this crisis. In responding to these problems, single-sex education merits reconsideration.

More importantly, the study of mixed- and single-sex schooling leads directly into the study of youth cultures, and their impact on the outcomes of education and school reform. It leads also toward a host of questions regarding recalcitrant gender segregation and gender stratification in coeducational schools. Many people will prefer to cling steadfastly to a set of taken-for-granted assumptions about the obvious superiority of coeducation. This book marches into relatively uncharted and rocky terrain. It poses some questions and implies many others. Although I do attempt to answer some of these questions, I would emphasize that the real work on this issue lies ahead. We need better data and more interest and debate.

Acknowledgments

The impetus for this project is entirely serendipitous. It began in 1981 while I was a postdoctoral fellow at Johns Hopkins University under a National Institute for Mental Health (NIMH) grant. As part of my training there, I became familiar with two large national educational surveys sponsored by the National Center for Education Statistics (NCES). During the spring of 1981, a great deal of attention focused upon a study of Catholic and public schooling that drew upon one of these data sets, High School and Beyond (HSB) (see Coleman, Hoffer & Kilgore, 1981). Sometime during 1982–83, I began work on a similar comparison of Catholic and public schools using the other NCES data set, the National Longitudinal Study (NLS). I did not finish this analysis, because in the process I came face-to-face with the fact that Catholic secondary schools were of two distinct types — about 42 percent of them were single-sex institutions and the remainder were mixed-sex.

Were it not for my postdoctoral study at Johns Hopkins, this book could not have been written. It was there that I finally was able to look over the edge and view the empirical side of sociology. Although some of my friends and colleagues may disagree with the results and/or the strategy of the analyses in this book, I remain forever grateful for the opportunity provided at Johns Hopkins University. Doris Entwisle, Karl Alexander, and Edward McDill provided both the NIMH fellowship support and over-the-shoulder research training. I am also much indebted to Thomas Reilly and David Baker, friends and colleagues, who helped in those immeasurable ways of just being there to listen, clarify, or challenge my ideas.

Two other people associated with Johns Hopkins have also played an important role in this book. Aaron Pallas reviewed the manuscript at a very early stage, and provided the kind of exhaustive, honest, and constructive review that every writer hopes for, but hardly ever receives. Aaron's review led to an entire reorganization, and to a much better book. James S. Coleman was the first Chairperson of the Department of

Sociology at Johns Hopkins University. I never met him until long after I had finished my work there. In fact, we have met only once. Nonetheless, I thought it was appropriate to ask him to write the Foreword section of this book. Despite his multitude of projects and obligations, he agreed, and I am most grateful.

Throughout the entire life of the manuscript, Mary Rogers has remained relentless in her encouragement and help. Mary has read and edited each chapter of the book in meticulous detail. She has contributed both to the substance and the style of the manuscript. On several occasions, when deadlines seemed impossible to meet, she ensured that I met them. Her generous care has helped to transform the book into something exciting.

At Providence College, I have been most fortunate to have had assistance from many people. Edgar Bailey and Barbara Farrell of the Phillips Memorial Library have been most helpful in meeting the many requests that I have made for material that was difficult to locate. I am grateful also to Lynn Parker and Ken Coleman for their assistance in much of the data preparation and analyses. Eventually, manuscripts must be typed, and retyped, and I am very fortunate to have had the services of a first-rate secretary, Marcia Battle.

Along the way, there were others who had a hand in moving the book along, in one way or another. This list of people includes: Michael Forcier, Sally Kilgore, Rabbi Joseph Fisher, David Mooney, Edward Power, Ellen Pitzi, and Bethany Booth. Finally, I want to express my appreciation to copyeditor Myra Cleary, and to the entire staff at Teachers College Press. I am grateful to Sarah Biondello, Susan Liddicoat, Nina George, and Mel Berk for their help and support in the development of the final product.

As is often the case, the bottom-line support team is one's family. For me, this is my dear wife and life-long friend Arline, and my daughters Julie and Kate. Arline is a wise and generous companion. Her insightful ideas are reflected throughout the book. I dedicate this book to Kate and Julie, in part because of their patience and love during the years it took to write the book, but most of all, because of all the time it took to *learn how to* write it.

As much as I might wish otherwise, I must release all these people from any obligations in defending the book, its purpose, its errors, and/or its conclusions.

CORNELIUS RIORDAN
PROVIDENCE, RHODE ISLAND
MAY 29, 1989

ONE

Gender Context and Educational Equity

If there is any misleading concept, it is that of coeducation.

—ADRIENNE RICH, 1979

Most Americans take coeducation for granted. Typically, their own schooling has been coeducational; often, they have little awareness of single-sex schools. Our political culture reinforces the taken-for-granted character of American coeducation. It implies that schools reflecting the variety of society exemplify what is best about democratic societies. Mixed-sex schooling mirrors life in society. From that viewpoint single-sex schooling is aberrant.

Rosemary Deem (1984) cites a friend's reaction to her research on coeducation.

> Oh . . . I hope you're not going to end up advocating those dreadful single-sex schools. . . . Awful places. . . . I went to one myself. . . . It took me years afterwards to adjust. . . . I couldn't relate to men at all when I left school. (p. xi)

Over the past years, as I worked on this book, I received similar reactions from both men and women. Particularly for people who went to single-sex schools, coeducation signifies interpersonal freedom and healthier human relations. Interestingly, both ex-students and teachers feel that all students, but especially boys, behave better in mixed-sex schools. In fact, there is a sense of mistrust or suspicion about single-sex schools.

Many people also take for granted that coeducation provides equality of educational opportunity for women. Like racial and ethnic minorities, women have long been excluded from the educational process.

1

Thus, many people regard coeducation as a major milestone in the pursuit of gender equality. Single-sex education, by contrast, appears regressive, possibly an anachronistic affirmation of the principle that schools can be "separate but equal."

Even educational researchers for the most part take coeducation for granted. Coeducation stands among their least studied topics. It takes a backseat to other questions about mixing or separating students in schools, particularly questions about race and social-class integration and ability grouping. The pros and cons of mixed- versus single-sex schooling, on the other hand, get little attention in most societies. In fact, researchers join the general public in taking for granted that the topic of segregated or desegregated schooling refers only to race.

Perhaps the main reason people commonly take coeducation for granted in our society is that the policy of coeducation has rarely been debated on educational grounds. Instead, the practice has most often evolved on economic grounds. Kolesnik (1969) notes:

> The question of whether [girls] should be educated together, or apart from, boys at the elementary level was resolved not so much on the basis of any principle so much as it was by economic necessity. Particularly in the smaller towns the establishment of the two schools, one for each sex, simply was not feasible. (p. 86)

Yet, as Robert Seybolt (1925), a noted historian of colonial America, points out:

> The legal attitude toward the education of girls in colonial America was highly conservative. In general, public provision was lacking; town schools were, in most cases, established especially for the education of boys. Some few towns, however, did permit girls to attend the elementary schools, either with the boys, or at "separate" hours. (p. 69)

Generally, girls attended when the boys were not present; that is, "early in the morning, late in the afternoon, during certain days of the week or certain months of the year, usually the summer months" (Kolesnik, 1969, p. 85).

How long this practice might have continued is hard to say. M. Carey Thomas (1900), an early president of Bryn Mawr College, notes:

> It was a fortunate circumstance for girls that the country was at that time sparsely settled; in most neighborhoods it was so difficult to

establish and secure pupils for even one grammar school and one high
school that girls were admitted from the first to both. (p. 322)

Thomas goes on to illustrate the "illiberal attitude" toward girls' education. In heavily populated districts like Boston and Philadelphia, girls
were unable to get a public high school (coeducational) education until
1878. Remarkably, Boston Latin School remained a boys' institution
until 1972 (Mulligan, 1985), as did Central High School in Philadelphia
until 1983 (Wilson, 1983).

In this manner, coeducation emerged and took root in America. And
this pattern exists worldwide. Reviewing a UNESCO study of 105 countries,
Greenough (1970) notes that "true coeducation is introduced initially much
more often as a result of particular circumstances than because of any
clearly defined principle" (p. 31). Thus coeducation evolved as a common-
place norm, not because of educational concerns as much as because of
other forces. Its taken-for-granted character stems from lack of debate over
the advantages and disadvantages of coeducation.

GENDER CONTEXT POLICIES

In America, boys and girls have usually attended the same public
schools. This practice originated with the "common" school. Of course,
at an early point in our society only boys received an education. Somewhat later, the only education for either boys or girls was single-sex
schooling, whether public or private. Once mass and state-supported
public education was established, however, it was clearly the exception
for boys and girls to attend separate schools. By the end of the nineteenth century, coeducation was all but universal in American elementary and secondary schools (Bureau of Education, 1883; Butler, 1910;
Kolesnik, 1969). The passage of Title IX of the Educational Amendments in 1972 virtually mandated that American public education be
coeducational and climaxed the institutionalization of coeducation in
American society.

Most private schools began as single-sex institutions. As recently as the
1978–79 academic year, 11 percent of all elementary and secondary private
school students attended single-sex institutions, with equal proportions of
males and females (Nehrt, 1981). Among secondary schools, however, about
34 percent of all private school students attended single-sex schools. During
the 1978–79 academic year, about 42 percent of all Catholic high schools
were single-sex (Coleman, Hoffer, & Kilgore, 1982).

Higher education in America began and remained all-male well into the nineteenth century. In response to this lack of equal opportunity, women's colleges opened in the 1830s and 1840s, initially as secondary-level "seminaries," which only later gained degree-granting status. Despite the fact that coeducational colleges began at about the same time (in 1833 Oberlin College was the first to make no distinction with regard to sex), women's colleges continued to prosper and grew in number until the middle of the twentieth century. Since that time, a major structural transformation has occurred in the higher education of women. In 1960, there were 268 women's colleges in America. Today less than 100 remain in operation. The current enrollment of 125,000 is about one-half of what it was in 1960 (Ingalls, 1984). Table 1.1 and Figure 1.1 illustrate this shifting pattern of single- and mixed-sex institutions of higher learning.

In contrast to the United States, coeducation in England and Ireland is recent. It was not until the beginning of the twentieth century that British elementary education became free, compulsory, and state supported (Deem, 1978). Before that, education was primarily private and only for boys from the aristocratic and upper classes. The Education Act of 1944 provided free and compulsory secondary education. It reorganized secondary schools into "comprehensive schools" designed to equalize educational opportunity by offering an alternative to the highly selective single-sex grammar schools. Comprehensive schools, attended mostly by working-class children, are coeducational.

Currently, most primary schools in England are coeducational. Yet one-third of state secondary schools and most private (or independent) schools remain single-sex (Byrne, 1978; Deem, 1978). The British situation contrasts with that in the United States in two critical ways. First, England still has a substantial number of private and state-supported,

TABLE 1.1.   U.S. Institutions of Higher Education
by Sex Status, Selected Years 1870 to 1982

Year	Number of Institutions	% Men Only	% Women Only	% Coeducational
1870	582	59	12	29
1890	1082	37	20	43
1910	1083	27	15	58
1930	1322	15	16	69
1960	2028	12	13	75
1970	2573	6	8	86
1982	3253	3	4	93

Sources: Grant & Lind (1973, p. 91); Newcomber, M. (1959, p. 37); Grant & Snyder (1983, p. 106).

FIGURE 1.1.   Coeducational and Single-Sex Institutions of
Higher Education in the United States, 1961-62 to 1981-82

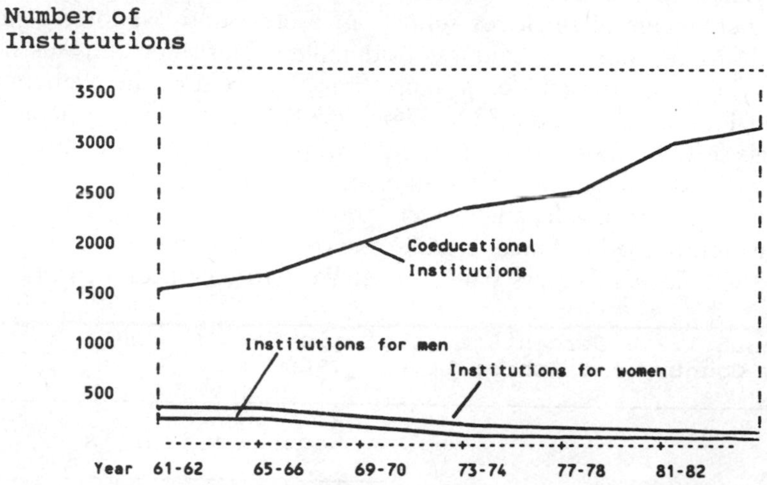

Number of
Institutions

Source: Grant & Snyder (1983, p. 106).

single-sex schools. Second, their existence has begun to stimulate research and debate (Deem, 1984; Shaw, 1976, 1980). A similar situation
exists in Ireland and Australia (Carpenter & Hayden, 1987; Hannon et
al., 1983).

The trend toward coeducation generally holds worldwide, although
some countries are considering a return to single-sex schooling.
Greenough (1970) summarizes the findings from a global UNESCO study
of coeducation.

> Of 105 countries which replied . . . 27 reported they now have a com-
> plete coeducational system . . . and the majority of other countries
> said they have mostly mixed establishments at different levels. . . . 14
> more countries said they were considering the introduction or devel-
> opment of coeducation. . . . Completely and legally, separate educa-
> tion exists in only two countries replying. . . . [Two others] said they
> were contemplating discontinuing coeducation and reintroducing
> separate classes. (p. 31)

It is significant to note, however, that the practice of coeducation inter-
nationally is far less prevalent when different school levels are considered.

A study of 19 countries by the International Association for the Evaluation of Educational Achievement (IEA) conducted in the 1960s provides a revealing analysis (Comber & Keeves, 1973). Table 1.2 shows the percentage of single-sex schools in each country at three school levels. Many countries exhibit considerable inconsistency. In Australia and England, for example, no more than 5 percent of the elementary schools are single-sex, but 32 to 47 percent of the secondary schools are single-sex. Of Western countries, only Belgium is consistently more single-sex at all levels. Chile, India, Iran, and Italy also support considerable single-sex schooling. Japan, Sweden, and the United States are the most consistently coeducational. Despite the overall movement toward coeducation, Table 1.2 shows that even in Western countries a substantial

TABLE 1.2.   Percentage of Single-Sex Schools by Country and School Level, 1969

| | | Secondary Schools | |
| | | | |
Country	Primary or Elementary	Primarily Students to Compulsory Level	Primarily Students to Terminal (Pre-University) Level
Australia	–	32	47
Belgium (Fl)	77	73	88
Belgium (Fr)	64	65	38
Chile	43	55	69
England	5	33	44
West Germany	1	10	46
Finland	3	8	16
France	–	–	34
Hungary	1	4	10
India	23	35	53
Iran	94	59	73
Italy	21	38	21
Japan	0	0	–
Netherlands	13	59	18
New Zealand	–	38	46
Scotland	5	9	20
Sweden	0	0	1
Thailand	9	49	17
United States	0	7	7

Source: Comber & Keeves, 1973, Tables 4.4, 4.5, 4.6.

percentage of schools remains single-sex. In fact, about 34 percent of the 19 secondary school systems are single-sex.[1]

Single-sex education assumes various forms throughout the world.

> In many countries, this consists of separate schools and school systems for boys and girls. Elsewhere, pupils may be separated by sex within schools for coursework, as a result of school policy or students' choice of electives. And finally, de facto segregation occurs partially, if not completely, in areas of certain grade levels where one sex or the other does not attend school. (Finn, Dulberg, & Reis, 1979, p. 494)

As was the case in the United States 300 years ago, in many countries girls and women are partially or entirely excluded from formal schooling, creating a single-sex situation by default. Counselors and teachers may also help to create de facto sex-segregated classes by channeling students of one sex into certain types of courses and activities. Coeducation in our society often reflects the play of processes other than strictly educational debate and policy making.

STUDYING MIXED– AND SINGLE–SEX SCHOOLING

Assessing the relative advantages and disadvantages of single-sex and mixed-sex schooling is difficult. Two stubborn obstacles are the enormous disparity in the physical facilities of the two types of schools and the substantial differences in the socioeconomic backgrounds of the students attending each type. Generally, mixed-sex schools provide better physical facilities, whereas single-sex schools enroll students from higher socioeconomic status homes. There are exceptions to this pattern, however, which further complicate the problem. For example, girls in Catholic single-sex schools in America are below average in socioeconomic status (see Chapters 4 and 5).

An additional problem is that mixed-sex schools may, at least initially, attract less talented students. Although empirical support for this contention is lacking, it seems reasonable that academically weaker students may lean toward a coeducational school, if only for certain social benefits. Any analysis of single- and mixed-sex schooling must somehow control for these factors. Unfortunately, such controls are often absent.

The most ambitious analysis of the effects of single-sex schooling is the IEA project mentioned earlier (Comber & Keeves, 1973; see also

Husen, 1967, 1974). It began in the mid-1960s with a study of mathematical ability. From 1966 to 1973, IEA examined 6 other school subjects in 21 countries. Identical tests and questionnaires were developed and translated into several languages. Another major research effort on single- versus mixed-sex schooling is Dale's 1966 British study. Dale (1971, 1974) examined the test scores, attitudes, and behavior of 2240 boys and girls in 42 mixed- and single-sex schools at both the 11- and 15-year-old age levels. Both of these studies are reviewed in Chapter 3.

Research on gender context in the United States has generally been limited to the college level. The most comprehensive study of gender context in American higher education is the Cooperative Institutional Research Program initiated in the late 1960s (Astin, 1968, 1977). This longitudinal investigation involves 200,000 students in more than 300 colleges and universities of various types. In this ongoing project, first-year students take a battery of tests, and selected samples of students are retested at graduation and during early adulthood.

Over the past several years, I have conducted three major studies of single- and mixed-sex schooling in the United States. This research is based on the highest quality data of school outcomes currently available, the National Longitudinal Studies of the High School Classes of 1972 (NLS) and 1982 (HSB). This research was undertaken to determine the effects of single- and mixed-sex schooling among both high school and college students in America, and, more important, to estimate these effects after statistically controlling for both home background and initial ability. This work forms the basis for Chapters 4, 5, and 6.

These and many other studies, executed within and beyond the United States and examining a range of educational levels, show that the structure of schooling has different effects on the educational outcomes of males and females. More specifically, the data suggest that the gender context of schooling is a consequential factor affecting what males and females derive from their schooling. These studies indicate that females especially do better, academically, in single-sex schools, across a variety of cultures. Moreover, the higher education research shows that "students at single-sex colleges are much more satisfied than students at coeducational colleges with virtually all aspects of college life" (Astin, 1977, p. 232).

COEDUCATION UNDER SCRUTINY

Gradually, critical concerns about coeducation have arisen. In the United States such concerns derive partly from the success of women in single-sex colleges; the results of experimental programs for girls; a decade or more of research suggesting girls may be seriously disadvantaged in mixed-sex settings of all types; and, perhaps most significant, the declining tenability of the assumption that racial minorities learn best in desegregated classrooms. I touch briefly here on some pertinent data, saving most of the findings for a comprehensive review in Chapter 3.

Although Title IX makes it difficult to conduct single-sex classes, even as pilot or experimental programs, several single-sex projects operating within the law have shown promising results for female students. In 1971, the Johns Hopkins University Study of Mathematically Precocious Youth began identifying mathematically talented children and promoting their talents through extracurricular educational experiences. Early results indicated that the coeducational program was more successful with boys than with girls. In an attempt to remediate this inequity, an experimental program for girls only was started. The project has been remarkably successful in bringing the progress of the girls toward parity with that of the boys (Brody & Fox, 1980).

At the University of Missouri–Kansas City, one section of a mathematics course is for women only. Women attending that section got higher grades and had a better completion rate than women in the mixed-sex classes of the course. Significantly, 56 percent of the women in the single-sex class enrolled in another mathematics course, compared with only 17 percent of the women in the other sections (MacDonald, 1980).

Similarly, data on classroom organization and climate suggest that females may be generally disadvantaged in mixed-sex settings. Most of the pertinent research is experimental, conducted either in classrooms or laboratories and including both elementary and secondary school teachers and students. Surveying the relevant studies, Lockheed and Klein (1985) conclude:

> Sex inequities characteristic of the larger society are found in abundance in coeducational classrooms; the most common of these inequities are . . . sex segregation, sex-stereotyped teacher–student interaction, and imbalanced cross-sex peer interaction. (pp. 189, 207)

Male students generally receive more attention from teachers and dominate discussions and classroom interaction at all levels.

Lockheed (1976) also notes that:

> Sex differentiated instruction under the guise of coeducation is the norm, rather than the exception. . . . Regretfully, equity of educational benefits are no more a natural consequence of coeducational class-

rooms than they are of [racial] desegregation. In both cases, simply placing boys and girls or blacks and whites together in a classroom — without specific intervention — may do as much harm as good. (p. 4)

Recent findings about the experiences of female students at coeducational institutions of higher learning support the notion that mixed-sex schools fail to provide equal educational opportunities for both men and women. Hall and Sandler (1982) argue that American coeducational colleges provide a "chilly classroom climate," which "puts women students at a significant disadvantage" (p. 3). Among other things, they found that the "chilly climate" discourages female students from participating in class, dampens career aspirations, undermines their self-confidence, prevents them from seeking help outside of class, and causes them to drop or avoid certain "sexist" classes. By contrast, students at women's colleges report higher self-confidence, greater involvement in both classroom and extracurricular activities, greater satisfaction with their college experiences, and higher occupational aspirations (Astin, 1977; Ingalls, 1985). Thus, it appears that the structure of schooling, especially its gender context, helps to create, maintain, and exacerbate sex differences in educational outcomes.

In England, substantial empirical evidence shows that British "girls are at a disadvantage if they attend a mixed school" (Shaw, 1984, p. 27). Finn (1980) shows that girls in mixed-sex schools score lowest of all students in both England and America. Ekstrom, Goertz, and Rock (1986) report that among American high school students in an academic track, standardized test scores for women declined more than scores for males during the period 1972 to 1980. "This differential decline reversed the lead that academic women had on the [1972] vocabulary and reading tests and increased the lead that academic men had on the [1972] and [1980] mathematics test" (pp. 75–76). Additional research (Department of Education and Science, 1975) suggests that girls' choices of subjects (chemistry and physics, for example) are less stereotypical in single- than in mixed-sex schools. Furthermore, in mixed-sex schools boys may use girls as a negative reference group in the academic realm, with negative effects on girls' own performance (Shaw, 1980).

The challenge is to eliminate or dramatically reduce the effects of social stereotypes in the classroom. Lockheed and Klein (1985) suggest with some reservations that "single sex education offers a possible alternative" (p. 211). Similarly, in the *Handbook for Achieving Sex Equity Through Education*, Klein (1985) advocates "research to determine if and when it is ever effective to have single sex instruction to achieve equitable outcomes" (p. 508).

Yet the study of single- and mixed-sex schooling goes beyond the question of which type is more effective. It encompasses the global problem of gender stratification. The issues involve both the persistent subordination of women and the extent to which schooling can change their subordinate status. Supporters of coeducation have argued that it, not single-sex schooling, provides the best chance of offering women and men equal education.

It is informative to note that currently the value of a *racially* desegregated classroom has become controversial and questionable. Racial integration (coeducation, that is) may not promote "learning among black children and, indeed, seems to hinder black achievement nearly as often as it helps" (Walberg, 1985, p. 24). The effects of desegregation are small, inconsistent, and/or inconclusive (Ascik, 1984; Green, 1984; National Institute of Education, 1984). (For an opposing view on the effects of desegregation, see Braddick II, Crain & McPartland, 1984; Crain, Mahard & Narot, 1982.) Overall, only 62 percent of the comparisons between desegregated and segregated classrooms show that desegregated groups are more effective for black children. Walberg (1985) suggests this difference is small in view of other educational practices that almost invariably yield positive results. Fleming (1984) reports that such findings hold for college students as well. She found that even though the black colleges in her sample are academically inferior to the white colleges by most measures, black students in predominantly black colleges showed more academic progress than their counterparts in integrated colleges (see also Curwood, 1986). This has led educators and parents in school systems such as Milwaukee and New York State to re-explore the potential of separate forms of schooling (Raspberry, 1987; Uhlig, 1987).

Increasingly, then, the data raise the fundamental question of whether or not coeducation can reliably provide a race- or sex-equitable classroom. Critics of coeducation argue that it is ideologically egalitarian but effectively inegalitarian. Shaw (1984) observes that "whereas coeducation in principle offers equality of opportunity but in fact reduces the opportunity of equality, single sex schools may offer genuine equality of opportunity in the highly unequal society in which we live" (p. 35).

Strong grounds exist for thoroughly reconsidering the possible advantages of single-sex schooling. Caution is in order, however. Single-sex education remains a hazardous topic, partly due to the fear that it may undercut hard-won gains in education for women. Some people feel the idea is irretrievably reactionary and unacceptable. The idea of single-sex (segregated) education lies uncomfortably close to controversial educational practices like selective and denominational schooling, parental choice, and tuition tax credits. Some feminists may contend that "separatism" is likely to have broader negative implications for other women's issues.

Studies of single-sex and mixed-sex schooling cannot skirt such misgivings. Yet as Lockheed and Harris (1984) remind us, sex segregation is the informal reality in most classrooms and schools, notwithstanding the improvements wrought by Title IX. Since sex segregation lies at the core of most coeducation, single-sex schooling should not be written off as a relic of the past. In the face of stubborn gender stratification, achieving educational equity between men and women is a challenge we dare not dodge.

OVERVIEW

The studies to date imply the need for a double-edged approach to questions about the relative merits of single- and mixed-sex schooling. On the one hand, the existing data provide a basis for describing the social psychology of single- and mixed-sex schooling. On the other hand, the data offer grounds for advocating a policy of single-sex schooling. I take on that twofold challenge in this book. My purpose is to show how educational institutions can become more fully responsible for and more consistently responsive to both their male and their female students.

Chapter 2 provides a brief history of coeducation and single-sex schooling, with emphasis on the United States and selected European countries. Chapter 3 reviews the arguments for and against mixed- and single-sex schooling. Chapters 4, 5, and 6 describe the empirical data and analyses of mixed- and single-sex Catholic schools in the United States. These analyses rely on national samples of the high school graduation classes of 1972 and 1982. These studies report both short- and long-term outcomes, with attention to cognitive, attitudinal, and occupational variables. Chapter 6 also contains an analysis of the effects of single- and mixed-sex colleges in the United States.

Chapter 4 lays the groundwork for understanding the social psychology of the single-sex school and that of the mixed-sex school. Chapters 5 and 6 then compare the outcomes for students in those two settings. These chapters, which also examine the outcomes of female graduates from both single- and mixed-sex colleges, thus establish a basis for discussing how the social psychology of an educational organization affects its students.

Finally, Chapter 7 argues the case for a policy of single-sex schooling. It sizes up the educational advantages of single-sex schooling for students and delineates the larger cultural advantages of equalizing the education of the sexes. Thus, this last chapter synthesizes the findings from the preceding chapters and asks, What sort of policy makes educational and cultural sense in view of the social psychology and educational outcomes typical in single- and mixed-sex schools? The scales tip, I conclude, in favor of single-sex schooling. I argue against the wholesale closing of single-sex schools and for the creation of a small number of experimental single-sex schools (or classes) at various educational levels.

The Rise and Fall of Single-Sex Schooling

It is not an uncommon sight to see a school whose entrances are imprinted with the proscription: "Boys" and "Girls." Nor is it unusual to find children in mixed array spilling out of either doorway. Gender designations etched on coeducational institutions reveal the tradition of separatism in mixed-sex schools and suggest that the tale of schooling is neither simple nor resolved. In this chapter, the development of women's educational opportunities is examined from its barely discernible roots in the early years of civilization to its rapid expansion in the nineteenth and twentieth centuries.

ANCIENT SOCIETIES

The contributions of ancient Greece to a systematic education are profound. While examining the innovations of a formal curriculum in such areas as music and oratory, however, it is easy to lose sight of the fact that the pre-Hellenistic Greeks were devoted more to athletic than to intellectual training. The gymnasium and ephebium, which glorified physical and military expertise, were the dominant educational institutions. This did not lead to much enthusiasm for the education of women. In fact:

> The ancient Greek city has been called a "men's club," a warrior and seafaring community that excluded women from its inner circles. The Greek style of education tended to be a male-to-male tutorial, often involving a close personal, even sexual, relationship between an older

and a younger male ... mothers were generally considered unfit to teach their own children. (Sexton, 1976, p. 24)

But there were dreamers. Plato's utopian plan for education, though never implemented, carried the following assumption:

If the difference [between the sexes] consists only in women bearing and begetting children, this does not amount to proof that a woman differs from a man in respect of the sort of education she should receive. (Appel & Freeman, 1962, p. 129)

The Republic (Sterling & Scott, 1985) envisions the ideal society being governed by the most qualified persons, both male and female. Here, Plato suggests that girls and boys be educated together from the ages of 6 to 18. In later years, Plato apparently reconsidered the idea and advised equal, but separate, education, expressing an ambivalence that later became an issue of educational policy. In his *Laws*, Plato recommends the segregation of girls from boys at age 6 and instruction of boys by men, and girls by women (Kolesnik, 1969, p. 46).

Aristotle was more representative of the accepted Athenian view: "We should look upon the female state as being as it were a deformity, though one which occurs in the ordinary course of nature (Iglitzin & Ross, 1976, p. 9). As such, the education of girls took place entirely in the home within the confines of a domestic curriculum. Although Aristotle contributed far less to educational theory than Plato, Aristotle's position on the limited education of women is the one that prevailed.

Not all Greek women were poorly educated. Spartan women were held in slightly higher regard by the state and were allowed at least some physical training as a preparation for bearing strong sons. There is also some evidence of the existence of women's schools in the historical literature. One such was an academy of poetry, music, and dance operated by the sixth-century Greek poetess Sappho on the island of Lesbos. The curricular emphasis was on the study of beauty and wisdom, and the school took the form of a religious community that paid homage to the goddess of culture (Marrou, 1956). Another, rather remarkable exception to the rule were the *heterae* (ancient counterparts to "mistresses" or "concubines"), who used their position as companions to men of position in order to become educated and culturally knowledgeable. Some of these enterprising women even opened schools (Kolesnik, 1969, p. 44).

The Hellenistic period ushered in the development of schools as literary agencies. In order to preserve the treasures of classical speculative thought, educators created a literature to capture and transmit the ideas of the past masters. This led to important revisions in the curriculum of education and expanded opportunities for women. Power (1970) contrasts the pre-Hellenistic (early Greek) and the Hellenistic attitudes toward women's enfranchisement by the educational system.

> It may not be too much to maintain that in early Greece not only were girls not educated, but educational theory, apart from Plato's tongue-in-cheek prospectus, which could have made room for girls, made no plans for their participation in instructional programs. In this transitional age [the Hellenistic period], however, more educational opportunity was distributed a good deal more freely than heretofore, and girls were even permitted to go to the palaestra and gymnasium. (p. 112)

Roman civilization adopted many customs from Greek culture. Yet, it had deep-rooted traditions of its own, such as a strong affirmation of the family and the woman's role as "guardian and teacher of the young" (Sexton, 1976, p. 25). There is some degree of historical irony in the fact that women served society as "elementary" teachers long before being allowed access to the formal educational sphere as students.

MEDIEVAL EUROPE

The decline of Roman civilization, labeled by early scholars as the Dark Ages, was not entirely without light for women. This period saw an expansion of Christianity and, with it, the Christian view of women. Christianity offered women a more favorable role, assigning a great reverence to the figure of Mary, who, we might conjecture, provided some redemption for the crimes of Eve.

Moreover, the Church at this time, particularly in the West, was suspicious of the classics, and a mystical, intuitive understanding of Scripture became the accepted route to enlightenment. This fit the contemporary image of the female nature; and because it did not stress book learning, women were at no significant disadvantage. Not until the Reformation did religion demand scholarship of its members.

There was a clear need, however, for women to function as preservers and purveyors of the Faith. The instruction and indoctrination of children became a vital part of the domestic role, and a formalized system of education for women developed as a result. According to some estimates, women were more literate than men during this period (Sexton, 1976, p. 26), and the primary educational institution for them was the convent. Parish schools also admitted girls, but the monastic, palace, and cathedral schools were almost exclusively for boys. (However, the vast majority of boys in the Middle Ages did not have the opportunity to attend these schools.)

Convents trained not only postulants but also girls who did not intend to take religious vows. The third "R" was religion, but other matters were sometimes addressed.

> As was the case in the monastic orders for men, the Rules by which nuns lived usually required their learning to read and write, and in some of their cloisters fairly advanced instruction in the liberal arts was available. (Kolesnik, 1969, p. 50)

Yet, opportunities for Christian women in education stood in sharp contrast to the role of women in the church hierarchy, where they were excluded from any positions of power and policy (McGrath, 1976). This had an important bearing on later and larger deficits in educational opportunities for women. As a system of higher education developed to produce an educated clergy, women were excluded from the most advanced forms of education because of their exclusion from the highest offices of the Church. At the end of the Middle Ages, some women were admitted to the great medieval universities (Sexton, 1976), but these were women of wealth and influence and were in no way representative of the general population.

Economic as well as religious influences affected women's education during this time. The guilds that developed during the Middle Ages offered women an avenue to some economic power in several ways. First, wives often worked conjointly with their husbands in cottage industries, which necessitated basic education in the industry and in business management. Furthermore, widows often assumed membership privileges in the guild after their husbands' death and appeared to have an equal voice.

> They helped elect officers and they took part in all proceedings. That women were far from passive members is evidenced by the guild rules that often forbade disorderly debates by both the "sisteren" and the "bretheren." (Sexton, 1976, p. 29)

There were also some exclusively female guilds, such as dressmaking, weaving, and other craft guilds.

THE RENAISSANCE AND REFORMATION

During the Renaissance, women not only enjoyed wider opportunity, but also made important gains in higher education. The schools most characteristic of the Renaissance, however, were grammar schools, which provided a humanistic curriculum for boys aged 10 to 16. In general, lower-class boys and all girls were excluded from these schools early in the fourteenth century, but developments in both single- and mixed-sex education emerged later during the humanistic revival.

Humanistic writer Juan Luis Vives favored the education of girls but felt that sex segregation was desirable. This theory was tested in several grammar schools founded by women in Florence and Paris, which proscribed the teaching of boys by women. One of the most famous schools of the Renaissance period was the Casa Giocosa of Vittorino de Feltre, and it was coeducational (Kolesnik, 1969). Despite its fame, however, it represented a departure from the educational policies of the era.

Despite the simulacrum of educational opportunity and attainment for at least the upper classes of girls and women, the term "Renaissance woman" did not bear the same meaning as "Renaissance man." The ideal woman of this time fulfilled a role best described as 'ornamental.' In 1598, an epistle addressed to the Lord Silueftre Cataneo by one Michel Bruto advised the lord on the education of his daughter. *The Necessarie, Fit, and Convenient Education of a Yong Gentlewoman* (Bruto, 1598/1969) is emblematic of the sixteenth-century paradigm for educating women of noble birth.

> I am not therfore of [the] opinion, in any sort whatsoeuer, that a yong gentlewoman should be instructed in learning & humane Arts . . . we account honestie & true vertue to bee more comely and a better ornament. (F8)
> The liberal arts belong properly to men that are civill and of good birth (H4) . . . [but for her] it ought to bee the more avoided, because the danger is great and lesse apparant. (H7) . . . yet I will not that shee should bee debarred from the commoditie of reading and understanding, because it is not onely commodious to a wife and vertuous woman, but a rich and precious ornament. (G4)

This parallels the French ideal of "femme au foyer," or the education of the ornamental woman in the charms of the foyer and the education of children.

More generally, education, male or female, was the privilege of the nobility and aristocracy, and women's education in all social classes was more restricted than men's. Kolesnik (1969) observes:

> For girls of the lower classes, the Renaissance brought about no signif-
> icant change in the European tradition regarding women's ability or
> educational needs. The barriers against feminine education had been
> dented, but it took the Reformation to initiate—if not in practice, at
> least in theory—the general concept of universal education for wom-
> en. (p. 53)

Humanism promoted liberal attitudes about the infinite possibilities of men; but if the possibilities of women were as limitless, the actualities of their daily existence often contradicted it.

The great religious upheavals in the sixteenth century greatly improved educational opportunity at all levels. The corruption of the Catholic Church and papal authority led to a distrust of its spiritual leadership. John Wycliffe's translation of the Bible from Latin into English in the late 1300s had given the common people access to the sacred word. This breakthrough was furthered by Luther's emphasis in the sixteenth century on the reading and self-interpretation of the Scriptures. A new ethic in both religion and education was embraced.

In 1559, the Lutheran state of Württemberg developed a public educational system jointly controlled by the Church and the state. This was the origin of "the ideal of universal, compulsory public education as we know it in the United States today" (Kolesnik, 1969, p. 53). For both boys and girls of the lower classes, free elementary schools were available. The style of the day was sex-segregated instruction in reading, writing, and religion. Boys of more favorable economic circumstances generally attended private schools in preparation for the university, and upper-class girls were generally tutored at home.

Protestantism in England did not lead to the formation of a public school system, and the private grammar school for upper-class boys became the dominant institution of this period for the Anglicans. The education of girls, though still within the confines of the home, now extended beyond the strictures of a domestic curriculum. Setbacks occurred, however, when Henry VIII, in the spirit of the Reformation, destroyed some of the monasteries and nunneries that had well-established educational programs for both boys and girls.

The Catholic reaction to Protestant religious and educational activities was the Council of Trent, which animated the Catholic Reformation and forged new directions in the education of Catholics. Several teaching orders emerged during this period, including the Ursulines (1534), who undertook the education of women in the Church, and the

Jesuits, founded in the same year, who specialized in secondary and higher education of boys. According to Kolesnik (1969) there were 200 Jesuit grammar schools across Europe by the year 1600.

THE ENLIGHTENMENT

The Age of Reason, by its very name, would seem to portend good things for women. The philosophical commitment of the era was to shed the light of reason on unexamined beliefs and unquestioned traditions. The beliefs and traditions surrounding women, however, did not yield easily.

The literary leaders of the period disagreed on the issue of women's enlightenment. English writer Daniel Defoe observed that "one of the most barbarous customs in the world . . . [is] that we deny the advantages of learning to women" (Kolesnik, 1969, p. 56). Rousseau, on the other hand, argued in *Emile* (1762) that "the whole education of women ought to be relative to men, to please them, to educate them when young, to care for them when grown, to counsel them, and to make life sweet and agreeable to them" (McGrath, 1976, p. 11). Education at this point in time was still primarily in the hands of the elite overseeing a private system of male education.

There were notable exceptions, however. In 1763 in Prussia, Frederick the Great mandated compulsory attendance for both sexes and oversaw the development of a two-track educational system. The first track consisted of the Volksschule and Mittelschule, publicly supported schools for the children of the common people, where boys and girls were educated separately not only in the basic skills but also in German literature, history, and geography. The second track consisted of the Gymnasium for upper-class boys, which was reminiscent of classical educational tradition, and the Lyceum for girls, which represented a secondary education (Kolesnik, 1969, p. 59).

EDUCATIONAL DEVELOPMENT IN ENGLAND
AFTER 1800

The development of education in Europe and America was quite different during the nineteenth and twentieth centuries. For this reason, it is useful to examine a European country in some detail. Each country, of course, has its own unique and important history. England, however, is especially useful as a comparison because (1) its educational expansion during this time is similar to that in the United States, and (2) the matter of single- and mixed-sex schooling has been addressed and debated in England perhaps more than anywhere else.

Nineteenth Century

The Victorian obsession with respectability and economic mobility restricted the education of women, at least for the middle classes. Education for middle-class women became emptied of practicality or productivity. Victorian gender assignments harked back to the "ornamental" role of women during the Renaissance.

Schools for women of means were small and private, and instruction often took place at home under the direction of a governess. The core of the curriculum was social, and the schools were primarily single-sex (Deem, 1978). Girls of the lower and working classes were given a more practical, basic education in the church schools, dame schools (run by older women in their homes), and industrial schools. Boys of the lower and working classes were educated similarly, often in a contiguous setting with the girls, but usually separated by a screen and by a curriculum that excluded the domestic arts. Until the last quarter of the nineteenth century, there were only a handful of schools for either class or either sex.

The 1870 Education Act required local school boards to provide elementary schools that would supplement existing forms of schooling. However, they could charge educational fees, which in effect prevented most working-class children from attending school. In England, free elementary education was not available until 1918 (Deem, 1978).

Deem (1978) documents the rise of domestic economy classes in Britain in the late 1870s and its impact on girls' studies. The number of girls taking domestic economy courses in elementary school in 1876 was 3307. By 1882, it had risen to 59,812. In 1890, a new course entered the elementary school curriculum dealing with "laundry work." "By the end of the nineteenth century sexual divisions in elementary education were clearly visible and the education of working-class girls was, if anything, more sex-specific than before 1870" (p. 11). The inclusion of domestic economy courses (cooking, laundering, and so on) in the schools, in England and elsewhere, almost certainly prolonged sex segregation either in the form of single-sex schools or single-sex classrooms.

Some progress occurred during this period, however, for middle-class women in "further" (as opposed to "higher") education. The governess/tutorial system, which had arisen to serve the educational needs of middle- and upper-class children, generated some interest in preparing middle-class women for teaching responsibilities. Emily Davies was a pioneer of this early form of teacher education. In 1869, Davies opened an experimental women's college in Hitchin, England. Despite great opposition, the college advanced the idea that women were capable of a higher education comparable to that offered by men's colleges. The few women's colleges in existence prior to this had offered women basically a secondary education and prepared them mainly for the teaching profession. Teacher training colleges were rigidly segregated by sex throughout the nineteenth century (Parry & Parry, 1974).

Teacher training presented both an avenue and an impediment to women seeking higher education. It institutionalized higher learning for women, while forestalling their access to a truly advanced education. Several women's colleges followed in the wake of Davies' experiment, and several tried (unsuccessfully) to affiliate with men's universities. The University of London, however, began admitting women to degree programs as early as 1878 (Burstyn, 1980). Despite the Bill of 1875, which allowed universities to grant women degrees, institutions like Cambridge did not take the initiative until 1948.

Twentieth Century

By the end of the nineteenth century, the rise in mixed-sex elementary and secondary schooling was assisted by new moral debates. Two proponents of coeducation in the early twentieth century were Alice Woods and the Reverend Cecil Grant. Woods was concerned with academic issues; Grant was motivated by the debate on morality.

> Grant and his supporters were so concerned with the "moral health" of boys that in order to counter the argument that co-education might lead to sexual relations between boys and girls, Alfred Parks, a teacher at Grant's Keswick school, maintained that even if this "evil" occurred, it would be less disastrous than the "moral ill-health" existing in single-sex schools. (Brehony, 1984, p. 8)

Two private schools were the forerunners of coeducation in England, Bedales (1893) and King Alfred (1898). They stressed the social rather than the academic benefits of mixed-sex schooling, including:

> the reduction of homosexuality amongst boys; less rough behaviour from boys subjected to the civilizing influence of girls; the replication of relationships within the family and adult world . . . [which would] help produce healthier marriages, and a wider choice of occupations for both sexes. (Deem, 1984, p. xiv)

Another factor stimulating the progress of coeducation was the expense of single-sex schooling, especially in rural areas. In 1902, 65 percent of British elementary schools were mixed-sex, although they fell into two categories. Dual schools educated boys and girls, but in separate environments, while true mixed schools educated them together (Brehony, 1984).

The Education Act of 1902 was, as Rosemary Deem argues, an important step in government endorsement and support of schooling, especially for the lower classes, but it was far from altruistic. Although it provided for educating working-class women for domestic service, it was nevertheless an important expansion of the educational system. In 1907, the Free Place Regulations made secondary schools for academically talented working-class students tuition free.

The 1902 Act established local school authorities charged with the responsibility of setting up secondary schools. In 1904, there were 184 secondary schools in England; by 1921, the figure had grown to 311 (Deem, 1984). Most of these (75 percent), however, were single-sex schools, reflecting far more traditional constraints on women's access to men's academic privileges than at the elementary level.

Some of the new high schools, however, were coeducational from the beginning, and a progressive movement in this area was clearly under way. Opposition to this development was not unanimously male. The Association of Headmistresses argued that girls would be disadvantaged by the presence of louder, more academically aggressive men and by the lack of occupational opportunities for women with coeducational training. Suffragettes Sophie Bryant and Maude Royden defended single-sex schooling on the basis that girls and women would bypass the academic intimidation imposed on them by boys and men, and that *feminine* interests would not be "sacrificed too much to the interests of boys" (Royden, 1919, in Brehony, 1984, p. 12).

Although the movement of women into coeducational situations was to some extent a social movement, until the 1920s the curriculum largely stressed domestic (household economy) and ornamental (art, music) subjects. Then the political and educational environment became more hospitable. English women were enfranchised in 1928 and began gaining limited access to universities and professions. The medical profession was among the first to be embraced by women seeking careers that required advanced education. The reaction from the male medical community was predictable, and the rationale for proscribing women's medical education was, suitably, medical. Many treatises on both sides of the Atlantic discussed the delicacy of the female constitution and the dangers posed to it by the rigors of a medical education. The professions most hospitable to women were social work, teaching, and nursing.

In the 1930s, educational research began to produce results favorable to the separation of the sexes, at least in curriculum. In *Sex and Personality* (1936), Terman and Miles compared the psychometric testing of boys and girls, finding

> a dichotomy of interests between boys and girls. Whereas boys had strong interests in exploits, adventure, out-door and physically strenuous activities, machinery, tools, science and inventions, girls preferred domestic affairs, aesthetic objects, sedentary and indoor activities, and looking after other people. (in Deem, 1978, p. 26)

The Education Act of 1944 opened both elementary and secondary education to all children without tuition or examination. The legislation carried an ambitious agenda of equal access, an agenda difficult to accomplish on both the gender and class level. In fact, class issues were of more concern than equality of the sexes, at least in the years immediately following the passage of the act.

After World War II, England experienced an increase in female labor force participation and in the diversity of women's work. The war effort had called on women to assume many of the responsibilities of men, and the postwar prosperity ensured their continuation in the labor force. Yet the wartime image of Rosie the Riveter gave way to nostalgic versions of the woman's role: mother, nurturer, homemaker. Popular culture reinforced the image, even though in reality women were to a great extent still employed. Unfortunately, the popular image rather than the practical reality of women's roles shaped the curriculum in the 1950s.

Several factors affected the access of women to higher education and the professions in the 1960s and 1970s. First, the postwar baby boom had created a shortage in the teaching force, and women once more were called upon to serve in the elementary schools. Second, the 1960s saw a tremendous expansion of the social service professions. The comprehensive school movement took root within this context, attempting to redress the wrongs of single-sex schooling and class-segregated curricula.

The expansion of coeducation in England in the twentieth century and the legislative initiatives that fostered the experiment derived, in part, from developments on the other side of the Atlantic. American educational theory and practice also emerged from Western tradition, but America was somewhat less constrained by the conservativism of that tradition than was Europe. The unique path of education in America from the colonial period, through the early republic, and into the twentieth century is central to our survey.

EDUCATION IN THE AMERICAN COLONIES

American education is rooted in the Protestant revolt, in which education was deemed necessary for the individual to understand and interpret Scripture. Kolesnik (1969) notes that within "a decade or two after landing in the American wilderness, they [the colonists] had established town schools, a Latin grammar school and even a college, Harvard" (p. 68). Girls, however, usually received no formal education and often were unable to read with any degree of proficiency.

The Puritans espoused the Calvinist principles of predestination and the image of human nature as fundamentally weak and evil. They had particular misgivings about the nature of women, regarding them with a degree of mistrust that reached its greatest expression during the witch trials of the 1600s. Nevertheless, the Puritans carried with them the reformation imperative of a literate congregation. Educational philosophy at this point was the handmaiden of religious doctrine, and women were still viewed as spiritual instructors.

In 1647, the Massachusetts Bay Colony passed the "Old Deluder Satan Act" requiring every town of 50 families or more to support a schoolmaster (Kolesnik, 1969, p. 69). In 1692, Virginia and Massachusetts enacted a law requiring heads of households to assume responsibility for the education of their families. The commitment to schooling, however, seems to have predated these injunctions; Boston Latin was founded in 1635 as the first boys' high school. As noted earlier, it remained a single-sex school until 1972.

Provision for higher education was nearly coterminous with settlement. Harvard was founded in 1636, and other colleges soon followed: William and Mary (1693), Yale (1701), Princeton (1746), Columbia (1754), Pennsylvania (1755), Brown (1764), Rutgers (1766), and Dartmouth (1769). The raison d'être of higher learning in the colonies was the production of an educated clergy, which meant that women were excluded. Yet, a relatively liberal policy of admission granted the benefits of a higher education to more men of modest means than the British system did. Women were more fortunate at the lower school level, where the ecclesiastical imperatives were supported by church schools open to both girls and boys. Not until 1789, however, were girls admitted to Boston public schools (Draper, 1909, p. 262). Although college was proscribed for women at this time, it is clear that it was nearly as unattainable for men (Solomon, 1985, p. 2).

Although the Catholic population at the time of the American Revolution numbered only 27,000 (Bowler, 1933, p. 8), a Catholic counterpart to the Puritan educational initiatives emerged during this period. Catholic schools for boys were established as early as 1634 by the Jesuits in Maryland (Dupuis & Craig, 1963). The Ursuline Academy, established in New Orleans with the support of the French Catholic Church in 1727, became the first exclusively girls' school in the colonies. The curriculum covered reading, writing, arithmetic, industrial training, and doctrinal instruction. An important development was the establishment of teacher training at this Catholic academy, which was certainly the earliest American ancestor of the normal school.

Economic demands in the growing colonies provided an additional impetus for literacy. City dwellers were heavily engaged in trade and commerce, and colonial women were often deeply involved in the management of family businesses. Despite the "literacy gap" between males and females of the same social class, Kerber (1987) concludes that "New England women in the years of the early republic were the most literate women in Western society" (p. 40). In tracing the origins of educational opportunity, these early developments provide the preconditions for equality of access.

To accommodate the expanding school-aged population, "paraschools" took root in the homes (often the kitchens) of older women in the community and became known as dame schools. Here, both boys and girls gained basic literacy, although the limited and informal nature of the schools casts some doubt on their overall importance. Perhaps the most significant bequest of these schools was the establishment (however marginal) of women as teachers in colonial America.

The primary purpose of the dame schools was, however, to prepare boys for admission to the town schools, which remained closed to girls until the nineteenth century. Eventually, when girls were allowed to attend town schools, they commonly attended at different times of the day than boys, usually in the early morning or late afternoon. Other schools required girls to attend on days that boys did not attend; for example, during the summer months or on class holidays. Thus, the majority of town schools segregated the sexes to some extent and did not practice coeducation until the nineteenth century.

The Latin grammar school and college were also available to New England boys. Kolesnik (1969) comments that girls received only the most elemental education. Seybolt (1925), however, suggests that some girls did receive an extensive education, but that it was provided in private schools and boarding schools rather than public schools.

Until the last quarter of the eighteenth century, the Latin grammar school was the only educational option for boys wishing to pursue higher studies. The economic, social, and religious changes that occurred in the late eighteenth century, however, brought about the founding of a new institution for secondary education. In 1778, Phillips Academy was founded in Andover, Massachusetts, marking the beginning of the academy movement. The new academies offered a richer variety of courses than the Latin grammar school and provided an alternative to traditional studies. Several academies also opened for women, constituting the major institutions for women's higher education in the nineteenth century. These private academies were strictly single-sex, although they sometimes offered similar curricula to males and females. Although the academies broadened students' educational attainment and redefined the concept of secondary education, they were only for the wealthy. They were strictly private and selective, and did not serve the needs of the general population.

Thus, at the close of the eighteenth century the majority of male students attended dame schools for elementary instruction and then continued their education in town schools. More advanced male students continued on in academies or grammar schools, and possibly colleges. Female students also attended dame schools, and a small percentage went on to town schools. Some girls attended the emerging female academies, but women were not allowed in colleges. Education beyond the informal dame schools and sex-segregated town schools was single-sex and private, tailored for the children of wealthy upper- or middle-class families.

There was an undercurrent of discontent, however, which gained expression among some women of more prominent families during the colonial era. The English feminist Mary Wollstonecraft's A *Vindication of the Rights of Woman* (1792) had an influence on both sides of the Atlantic. In her writings, Wollstonecraft articulated the connection between women's confinement and their lack of educational opportunity and directed philosophical blows to those who would deprive women in this sphere. Her plans included a national commitment to coeducation and the entrance of women into the field of medicine as both doctors and nurses (Solomon, 1985). The only aspect of medicine open to women during the early years of the republic was the paraprofession of midwifery.

During the eighteenth century, the Quakers were the first to establish coeducational schools; by the late 1700s, several New England town schools began to develop summer programs for girls. These developed later into full-year schools, and tax revenues were used to pay female teachers (Kerber, 1987, p. 41). By 1784 in the town of Dorchester, Massachusetts, the Catholic Church had established a coeducational school offering a curriculum of reading, writing, and simple mathematics, which was gradually supplemented by French, history, geography, and needlework (Doyle, 1932).

NINETEENTH–CENTURY AMERICA

According to Phyllis Stock (1978), by the end of the eighteenth century, dame schools, town-subsidized schools, and religious schools were the basic means of education for most citizens, and they drew fewer girls than boys. The idea of a free, compulsory education (supported by tax revenues) was first proposed in America by Thomas Jefferson in 1779. Jefferson recommended three years of public education for both boys and girls in Virginia, but it was not until the next century, during his presidency, that his innovation took root. Between 1825 and 1860, the proposal to provide free primary education to all children, male and female, was hotly debated. Kolesnik (1969) notes that this issue was second in importance only to the slavery issue. Nonetheless, the idea of tax-supported education was generally accepted and institutionalized before the end of the nineteenth century.

The Common School

The type of tax-supported education that emerged in the early part of the nineteenth century became known as the "common school." Its name reflects the fact that it served the common people and had a common curriculum of the three R's and religion, with little individual variation. Although both boys and girls attended these schools, what resulted cannot be called true coeducation. As Kolesnik (1969) reports:

> The one-room district schoolhouse did not particularly lend itself to separation of the sexes, but in such schools the boys and girls were not uncommonly seated apart from one another and were segregated during recess or play periods. Coeducation, in brief, did not necessarily imply co-recreation, and heterosexual socialization was not only discouraged but strictly prohibited. (p. 86)

The reasons for tolerating coeducation in this form were often economic rather than educational, especially in sparsely populated areas, which could not afford to separately house students. Respondents to a Bureau of Education (1883) questionnaire often cited such economic necessity for the institution of mixed-sex education. Most towns could not afford two schools, so it developed that the sexes were educated together.

The Development of the High School

The only institutions resembling a high school before 1821 were the rare grammar schools and academies of the colonial period, which served as feeders of particular colleges. In that year, a public commitment to high school education was made in the form of the "English Classical School." In 1827, Massachusetts began requiring towns of 500 or more householders to establish this type of "high" school. The first public girls' high school opened in 1824 in Worcester, Massachusetts, and the first coeducational high school originated in Lowell, Massachusetts, in 1840 (Kolesnik, 1969, p. 87). Yet by 1860, there were only a few more than 300 public high schools in the United States (Blum et al., 1984).

Although female and coeducational high schools grew slowly before the Civil War, the pace was impressive thereafter. In 1880 there were nearly 800 American high schools; by 1890, over 2500; and by the end of the century, more than 6000, the great majority of which were coeducational (Kolesnik, 1969, p. 88). By 1882, the United States Commissioner of Education noted that 90 percent of the urban schools were coeducational.

Solomon (1985) reports that by 1890, more girls than boys graduated from high school (p. 46). This was largely attributable to the rapid growth of the common school and the need for an inexpensive supply of teachers. Gappa and Uehling (1979) report that by 1850, there were nearly "2 million school-age children requiring about 200,000 teachers, 90% of whom were women" (p. 5). City schools accommodated a rising immigrant population, and the growth in rural schools was accelerated by the settlement of the west.

By the end of the nineteenth century, both males and females could attend public elementary or common schools and high schools. Stock (1978) argues, however, that attendance at any of these public schools was low because compulsory education laws, when they did exist, were not effective. The majority of these schools were coeducational, but the option of attending single-sex public schools did exist in some larger cities in the east and south. The wealthy also had the option of attending various private institutions, which were primarily single-sex schools, though women's academies were losing ground as women were admitted to public schools on an equal basis with men. Of course, many students availed themselves of the various church-related schools, which had also experienced steady growth. Catholic and Jewish schools, especially high schools, were single-sex, while most Protestant institutions, especially Quaker schools, were mixed.

The Academy Movement

Coeval with the development of the public high school was the seminary (or academy) movement. Draper (1909) draws the following distinction between the function of the high school and the academy:

> The business of [the academy] was to serve the interests that were above [college] . . . that of [the public high school] is to help on the broader and more worldly concerns that are below. . . . The one was classical with some practicalities; the other is severely practical . . . with some classical appurtenances (pp. 153–154).

Although democracy and coeducation may have been best served by the high school, women's place in higher education was probably won by the academies.

The academy movement, led by Catharine Beecher, Emma Willard, and Mary Lyon, spawned institutions modeled after the English finishing school. Their original purpose was to provide a moral, literary, domestic, and ornamental education (Sexton, 1976). By 1850, over a quarter of a million students (men and women) were enrolled in over 6000 academies (Solomon, 1985). Doyle (1932) reports that "between 1819 and 1835, 32 academies were incorporated with the prefix 'Female' affixed to their titles" (p. 15).

The Catholic Church played an important role in the seminary movement. Following the Civil War, a group that later affiliated with the Visitation Order established an academy at Georgetown. Sr. Mary Marcella Bowler (1933) details the development of this academy into an institution for training young teachers with an impressive curriculum including chemistry, astronomy, poetry, languages, needlework, and domestic economy. This was soon followed by another academy of teacher training in Baltimore in 1870, founded by Elizabeth Seton. These seminaries supplied the teaching force for Catholic girls' schools such as those developed in Kentucky under the Right Reverend Benedict Joseph Flaget. From 663,000 in 1840, the Catholic population swelled to 3,103,000 in 1860 because of immigration (Shaughnessy, in Bowler, 1933), thus stimulating growth in church-sponsored education.

Astin and Hirsch (1978) regard the seminaries and academies as "glorified high schools" (p. 55), but Solomon (1985) defends the curriculum of these early female institutions.

> In addition to offering chemistry and physics, many, like Patapsco, excelled in botany and geology. . . . Although ornamental studies in drawing, singing, and piano playing became conventional offerings, most academies, contrary to public opinion, did not give courses in housewifery or domestic science. (p. 23)

Higher Education

Whether or not the early seminaries were collegiate in nature, their movement in that direction was certain. The first of these institutions to call itself a college was the Georgia Female College, founded in 1836, though it did not immediately award the bachelor's degree and was at first a college in name only. Mount Holyoke Seminary, established by Mary Lyon and chartered in 1836, offered an education so much beyond other seminaries in its scope that it is often regarded as the beginning of higher education for women. Another institution closely resembling a male college in its standards was the Elmira Female College, founded by a group of clergy and lay professionals in 1855 (Astin & Hirsch, 1978).

Following the Civil War, in fact, a renewed commitment was made to women's single-sex institutions in the form of endowments. In 1865, Matthew Vassar donated lands and money for a woman's college to be modeled along the lines of the traditional institutions for men (Solomon, 1985). In the next decade, Wellesley and Smith followed. Bryn Mawr opened in the fall of 1885 with a curriculum including English, science, history, and philosophy and an elective system patterned after the Johns Hopkins model.

Of course, all-male colleges had been established in the early years of the country, and they had continued to grow. The original Ivy League colleges were joined in the late nineteenth century by a host of Catholic, Protestant, city, and state universities. Many of these schools remained single-sex until the 1960s. Coeducation at the college level did arise during the mid-nineteenth century, however, largely because of economic necessity. As mentioned earlier, Oberlin began accepting qualified female students in 1837 and is the oldest coeducational college still in existence. Ohio State became the first state coeducational college in 1856. Within a few decades many midwestern universities were accepting women students.

The opening of college-level education to women split geographically in two directions. In the west, where money was needed to maintain the newly emerging colleges, coeducational institutions appeared as an economic solution. These colleges succeeded in increasing their intake of tuition by accepting women and hence enlarging the total enrollment. In the east, however, more prestigious colleges did not need to drastically stimulate enrollment, and many remained single-sex male institutions. In response, women's single-sex colleges began to develop in the east, as an extension of the academy tradition. Since coeducational colleges emerged less rapidly in the east, attending single-sex institutions was the only option to many women there. In any case, a U.S. Commissioner of Education report of 1891 indicates that over half of the colleges surveyed at that time were coeducational (Stock, 1978).

Another species of women's college arose in the latter half of the century. The "affiliated" colleges attempted, ultimately successfully, to attach themselves to prestigious male colleges. Radcliffe College developed through the Harvard Annex (1879), where the Society for the College Instruction of Women offered courses taught by Harvard professors. Not until 1893, however, was Radcliffe allowed to confer degrees, and it was 1965 before Radcliffe women were awarded the Harvard bachelor's degree. Examples of other coordinate arrangements are Barnard College, which affiliated with Columbia University in 1891; Pembroke, which affiliated with Brown University; and the H. Sophia Newcomb Memorial College, which became part of Tulane University in 1886.

Predictably, a concerted backlash arose against both female affiliation in higher education and the larger question of equal educational and professional opportunity. One reactionary spokesperson was Dr. Edward Clarke of Harvard University. In *Sex in Education: A Fair Chance for the Girls* (1873) he warns that female "periodicity" and delicacy proscribe the rigor of academic life. A male educational curriculum, he further claims, interferes with a woman's reproductive system. The book was so successful that in 1874 the Executive Committee of the National Education Association invited him to present a paper on the "Education of Girls" at its annual meetings. This address is often cited as indicative of the negative climate surrounding the coeducational movement. His half-hour address was later expanded to a book-length discussion entitled *The Building of a Brain*. Dr. Clarke hoped that the discussion that he began would continue "till Nature's fundamental distinctions are practically and permanently recognized in and out of school" (Clarke, 1874, p. 9). Clarke's position was severely criticized and refuted by teachers and physicians who pointed to a faulty methodology and logic. Unfortunately, these critiques were not widely circulated at the time (Seller, 1983). G. Stanley Hall was another denigrating voice in the reaction to the opening of higher educational opportunities for women. In his article, "The Kind of Women Colleges Produce," Hall railed against the ideals promoted at women's colleges, labeling them institutions for "glorified spinsterhood" in the hands of "misguided feminists" (Palmieri, 1987, p. 57).

Nevertheless, coeducation came to American higher education during the nineteenth century. Gappa and Uehling (1979) cite the declining enrollments during the Civil War as the major reason for opening the gates. In addition, the sparsely populated western states, which were dealing with the provisions of the Morrill Land Grant Act (1862), found it difficult to support a bifurcated educational system. Astin and Hirsch (1978) note that "it is generally agreed that the purpose of coeducation was not to raise the status of women but to assist the institutions economically" (p. 60).

Catharine Stimpson (1987) places the origin of the term "coeducation" in the United States in the 1870s: "It names our efforts to educate men and women in the same space, although rarely for the same place" (p. 155). In 1837, Oberlin College enrolled four women. Those women were excused from classes on Mondays to do laundry, and they took the "Ladies Course," which bypassed the rigors of the male curriculum. However, even feminist Lucy Stone, who demanded that women be allowed to read at the commencement exercises, placed the domestic duties in perspective and claimed that the men carried their share of these tasks (Ginzberg, 1987, p. 71). Under the banner of reform, Oberlin was racially as well as sexually integrated, and the unorthodox nature of these arrangements inspired the Ohio legislature to attempt to revoke its charter several times. Nonetheless, a tradition of separatism reflected itself at Oberlin in the alternate use of some of the facilities (most notably libraries), but this may have actually helped to make coeducation more palatable to the public.

Within a few years, other institutions followed the Oberlin model and opened enrollments to women. The next 20 years saw the opening of such colleges as Antioch in Ohio (under President Horace Mann), Syracuse, Bates, Grinnell, Swarthmore, and Knox. Solomon (1985) points out that many of these colleges were staffed with graduates of Oberlin. Boston University in 1873 became the only college in Massachusetts to admit women. Retrospectively, critics of these early coeducational colleges are in general agreement that male–female equality of educational and occupational opportunity was neither the purpose nor the reality of these schools (Schwager, 1987).

Harvard's president, Charles W. Eliot, firmly opposed coeducation, despite pressure from the female family members of alumni. The University of Chicago admitted women upon its opening in 1882, although William Rainey Harper attempted to segregate the classes when female enrollments multiplied geometrically. He succeeded in establishing a junior college in 1902 and segregating the upper divisions. Opposing him (unsuccessfully) was faculty member John Dewey (Solomon, 1985, p. 59).

An interesting development occurred in the west, where the Morrill Land Grant Act, which did not legislate a commitment to coeducation, stimulated the formation of state colleges. Women in these institutions were often admitted into the normal school of the university rather than into the larger institution. Normal schools became the new single-sex institutions at the close of the nineteenth century, channeling women into the "feminized" profession of teaching.

AMERICAN EDUCATION IN THE TWENTIETH CENTURY

By the turn of the century, the great expansion of education in America had begun. That expansion was almost entirely mixed-sex in character. This was true for both secondary schools and colleges, and for public and private schools. The rise of single-sex schooling for both men and women had come to an end.

Secondary Schools

By 1900, 98 percent of public high schools in America were coeducational (U.S. Commissioner of Education, 1901). Allowing for the full development of boys' and girls' trade schools during this century, and the maintenance of a few old, classic college preparatory schools such as Boston Latin and Central High School of Philadelphia, this figure remained stable until just recently. This is not to suggest that public debate on the issue was closed off, but only that the practice had been established. As noted above, however, the subject was never hotly debated, and, as Hansot and Tyack (1988) have noted, whatever debate there was on the topic has had little impact on the practice of coeducation.

Hansot and Tyack (1988) cite a variety of documentation that during the early part of the century, boys often dropped out of school, making schools somewhat single-sex by default. The apparent reasons for this were a combination of greater job opportunities for men and a sense that boys experienced discontent in the face of the academic success of girls. Hansot and Tyack (1988) also point out that during the

Progressive era, the comprehensive urban high schools became more specialized in their curricula, which, in turn, made gender differentiation more salient within coeducational schools. Driving this process, which, however, did not apply to rural areas, were the dual forces of vocational education and the psychology of individual differences. Few figures are readily available as to the actual male–female ratio in classrooms, but it would appear that well into the twentieth century there was considerable single-sex education going on in schools that were called coeducational. Even today, notwithstanding the mandates set forth in the Title IX regulations, vocational education remains primarily sex-segregated.

Hansot and Tyack (1988) also note that throughout this period, students in coeducational schools may have "experienced more gender differentiation in the informal cultures of the schools than in the official organization" (p. 758). This observation has been reported repeatedly, most recently by Lockheed and Klein (1985), and bears importantly on much of the remainder of this book. Within public school classrooms, however, mixed-sex schooling appears to have been the norm. Tyack and Hansot (1988, p. 40) "examined hundreds of pictures of 20th century classrooms in the photographic division of the Library of Congress. Typically, these show general mixing of the sexes in the academic classrooms that formed the basic school day for most students in high school."

By 1924, about 90 percent of high schools in America were under public control, reversing a statistic favoring private schools just a century earlier (Cole, 1928). This nine-to-one ratio of public to private schools has remained approximately intact to the present time (Nehrt, 1981). Of course, private schools were much slower to move toward coeducation. In 1924, more than 50 percent of all private high schools were single-sex institutions (Cole, 1928). In 1947, 46 percent of Catholic high schools still remained single-sex. However, these schools, being larger on average, enrolled about 62 percent of the total number of students (Mary Janet, 1949). This figure changed very little over the next three decades. During the 1978–79 school year, about 42 percent of Catholic high schools were single-sex (Coleman, Hoffer, & Kilgore, 1982), although this figure may be substantially lower today as a result of many school closings during the 1980s. Of these single-sex schools, about 60 percent are female and a greater proportion, which are mainly girls' diocesan schools, serve lower-income students (Bauch, 1988).

The vast majority of other types of private schools are coeducational. Although the data are difficult to come by, one can estimate that no more than 20 percent of all other types of private schools are single-sex institutions. Based on several surveys of all types of private schools in the late 1970s, Nehrt (1981) reports that about 34 percent of the students attended a single-sex high school (this figure is higher for Catholic school students, as noted above). Since Catholic schools made up about two-thirds of all private schools in these surveys, we can assume that the percent of single-sex schools of other types is less than 20 percent. Of course, these figures can be deceptive, because private schools enroll only about 10 percent of all students in the United States (Nehrt, 1981). Finally, these estimates may have decreased during the 1980s, especially since Catholic school enrollment has declined substantially (Cooper, 1988).

Higher Education

By 1900, most of the best-known women's colleges were well established. During the first third of the twentieth century, however, the number of single-sex colleges continued to grow. In many instances, former 'seminaries' became quality colleges for women. Examples of this transformation are Mary Baldwin, Judson, and Agnes Scott. Around 1930, Bennington and Sarah Lawrence opened as experimental women's colleges, offering a more innovative curriculum than the traditional schools.

As Table 1.1 in Chapter 1 shows, between 1890 and 1910, coeducational institutions of higher learning became the dominant type of college, having previously been the minority. In 1890, 43 percent of postsecondary schools were coeducational; by 1910 the figure had jumped to 58 percent. From 1890 onward, the percentage of single-sex colleges dropped from 57 to 7 percent in 1982. If only four- or five-year colleges are considered, however, that figure is 8 percent (Grant & Snyder, 1983).

Patricia Graham (1978) points out that college attendance for women as a whole, relative to men, actually declined significantly from 1920 to 1970. In 1920 women represented 47 percent of the national total undergraduate enrollment, but declined to an average of only 38 percent over the next five decades. Graham notes also that in the 1930s a record high of 32.5 percent of college presidents, professors, and instructors were women (see also Conway, 1974). This figure undoubtedly represents a high-water mark in the existence of women's colleges, and generally coresponds with the data displayed in Table 1.1 in Chapter 1.

As in secondary schools, coeducation was adopted in Catholic colleges at a much slower pace. In 1914, DePaul University admitted women on an equal basis with men, but as Power (1958) reveals, in most formerly all-male Catholic colleges, women were enrolled only on a part-time basis or during the summer until the late 1920s. Even as late as the 1950s, women in formerly all-male Catholic colleges were a token minority (Whelan, 1952). Of course, there were an ample number of women's Catholic colleges available throughout the century. The first Catholic women's college was the College of Notre Dame in Maryland, which was opened in 1896. Separate Catholic colleges for men and women remained the norm until the major transformation to coeducation during the 1960s and 1970s. At mid-century, two-thirds of all four-year women's colleges were Roman Catholic (Jencks & Riesman, 1968).

Since 1960, a major structural transformation has occurred regarding the higher education of women. In 1960, there were 268 women's colleges in America; today only 100 are left. The current enrollment of 125,000 is about half of what it was in 1960. Since the most prestigious and formerly all-male colleges embraced coeducation in the early 1970s, women's colleges have steadily lost applicants. Recently, however, the strength and vitality of the remaining core group of women's colleges appear to have been renewed. From 1974 to 1984, enrollments have grown by 25 percent (Ingalls, 1984). Nonetheless, for some schools, such as Goucher and Wheaton, it was too little, too late, and they have gone coeducational.

THE CO–INSTITUTIONAL SCHOOL

A middle ground emerged in the 1950s for those who recognized the advantages of combining single-sex and mixed-sex education. During that time, Catholic educators found in the co-institutional school a means of providing the benefits of both types of schools. Co-institutional schools

> have separate classes for boys and girls in separate wings (or sometimes on separate floors) of the same school building. The students are usually, but not always or necessarily, taught exclusively by instructors of their own sex and have their own counselors and advisors. Convenient to both the boys' and girls' areas of the building are such facilities as the library, cafeteria, gymnasium, auditorium, book store and administrative offices, which are used by both sexes. In the co-institutional school boys and girls have ample opportunity to mingle socially before, between and after classes and do work together on extra-curricular activities without leaving the building. (Kolesnik, 1969, pp. 35–36)

By 1965 more than 90 Catholic co-institutional high schools existed in the United States. The co-institutional school, or "dual" school, exists worldwide. Drawing upon data gathered during the late 1960s by the International Association for the Evaluation of Educational Achievement, Comber and Keeves (1973, p. 151) found that most countries offer at least some form of single-sex schooling, including some co-institutional schooling.

SUMMARY

Both historically and cross-culturally, the provision and organization of schools for males and females has followed a predictable pattern. Schools were established first for males only; females were excluded entirely. This was usually followed by separate schools for each sex, and finally, in some societies, by coeducation. Although the trend today is toward coeducation, there is considerable variation from country to country in the proportion of single- and mixed-sex schooling. Some countries offer single-sex classrooms within mixed-sex schools.

The question of whether single- or mixed-sex schooling is more advantageous, and for whom, is still unresolved. In many countries, such as the United States, it has been taken for granted that mixed-sex schools are preferable both socially and academically. The remainder of this book attempts to provide a close examination of the merits of both types of schooling, both theoretically and empirically.

THREE

The Pro and Con Arguments

Two rationales dominate the arguments about single- and mixed-sex schooling. One centers on the social benefits, and the other concerns the academic outcomes that students derive from single- or mixed-sex schooling. An example of the former is reducing invidious sex stereotyping; an example of the latter is equal educational attainment. Positive results in *both* the social and the academic spheres are not always possible. Inconsistent outcomes are typical, even though proponents of a particular school gender context (mixed- or single-sex) may argue otherwise. In this chapter I focus on the various arguments and empirical evidence that have been advanced about both the social and academic benefits of cach school type. In Chapters 5 and 6, I will reconsider some of the empirical outcomes with new data.

THE CASE FOR COEDUCATION

Economic Efficiency

As noted earlier in Chapters 1 and 2, "Coeducation was instituted in America on economical grounds, as in thinly populated districts it was found that the number of pupils was too small to admit of separate schools being provided for boys and girls" (Hawtrey, 1896, p. 41). Separate schools for boys and girls would have necessitated duplicating expensive facilities, equipment, and personnel, jeopardizing the very existence of some local communitites. Occasionally, in thickly settled areas, people challenged the educational value of mixed-sex schooling. Kiddle and Schein (in Hawtrey, 1896, p. 43) note that

in some of the larger cities, as the schools grew large, and were composed of children gathered from all classes of society, it was often
deemed best to organize separate boys' and girls' schools, especially as
this could be done without injury, but possibly with a benefit to the
classification.

Generally, however, coeducational schools, begun under the pressure of
economic necessity, survived long after the population could easily have
supported single-sex schools. Over time coeducation became commonly
accepted as the best way to educate young people.

Thus, in America at least, coeducation started not because of any
firm belief in its sound educational effect, but rather because of financial constraints. Even today economic considerations continue to mandate mixed-sex institutions among private schools, especially Catholic
institutions. In Providence, Rhode Island, for example, three single-sex
institutions recently merged to form a mixed-sex Catholic school. The
stated reasons for the change were largely economic (Dujardin, 1983).

The Natural Situation

A second case for coeducation presupposes that educating boys
and girls together is natural. Many parents and teachers think single-sex
schooling may obstruct the development of positive relations with members of the opposite sex. They also argue that boys and girls must learn
to live and work together. Quite specifically, some argue that coeducation is conducive to happier marriages (Hale, 1929). At least one investi-
gator has provided support for that contention (Atherton, 1972). From
this point of view separation of the sexes in school creates an unrealistic
situation.

Dale (1971, 1974), following his extensive study described in Chapter 1, concluded that British mixed-sex schools were more successful
than single-sex schools in almost every respect. Most of the data sup-
porting this contention are, however, attitudinal and social, not academic (Atherton, 1972; Campbell, 1969). Dale noted, for example, that students think mixed-sex schools provide a more pleasant atmosphere than
single-sex schools and that they were happier in mixed-sex schools. Predictably, Dale found that students preferred mixed-sex to single-sex
schools and that their most frequent reason was the overemphasis on
academic work and academic success in single-sex schools. Dale's work
thus suggests that coeducational schools place less emphasis on scholarship and achievement, and greater emphasis on affiliation and nonacademic activities. Whereas others may view nonacademic activities as

distracting, the coeducationalists see them as opportunities for developing the ability to relate positively with members of the opposite sex. Dale noted that boys' academic performance was higher in mixed-sex schools and that girls' was higher in single-sex schools. Nonetheless, he favors coeducation because of the improvement in boys' academic performance and the greater overall happiness, maturity, and social adjustment of both boys and girls in mixed schools.

One British critic (Shaw, 1980) labels Dale's interpretations "a sexist programme in the extreme."

> Not only are a "better adjustment" and a more "mature" attitude to members of the opposite sex seen to be a fair exchange for girls' academic achievements, but those measures themselves embody a commitment to and a reinforcement of the most traditional and limiting sex roles. The acceptable trade-off is supposed to be a poorer education for girls in favor of "happier" marriages for both sexes and even more sex-role stereotyping. (p. 69)

Spender (1982) agrees that boys' academic advantages at mixed-sex schools accrue at the expense of advantages for girls.

Some concerns also have been raised about the possibility of a homosexual orientation resulting from single-sex schooling. According to Sexton (1969):

> The sad lesson taught by boarding schools is that boys who are shut off from normal heterosexual contact tend to turn in on their own sex and find love objects there. Just as many farm boys find sex objects among animals, so will boarding-school boys find sex and love where it is available. . . . So it is in prison, ships, camps—wherever the sexes are separated for long periods. (p. 186)

Yet, only single-sex boarding schools separate boys and girls for long periods of time.

A middle line of reasoning holds that coeducation is acceptable in primary or elementary schools but not in secondary or postsecondary schools (Fisher, 1986; Sadler, 1903). Proponents of this view argue that during and after puberty mixed-sex schools provide many distractions deleterious to academic and/or social outcomes. This viewpoint rests largely on assumptions about the adolescent subculture (see below) or on religious grounds. An entirely different view is held by those concerned about the gap between males and females in elementary school, where girls consistently do much better academically than boys. According to Boocock (1980), "The apparent disadvantage of boys in the early elementary years has led to serious proposals that the sexes be separated for the first few grades and that systematic attempts be made to recruit more male teachers at this level" (p. 85).

Reduction of Gender Stereotypes

Some people contend that in separate schools boys and girls may acquire mistaken notions about the opposite sex. Stereotypes of males and females may be established and maintained, and the relative lack of intergroup contact would allow little opportunity to disconfirm such stereotypes. A third case for coeducation centers on reducing gender stereotypes.

Considerable knowledge is available regarding the effects of segregation and stereotyping in the area of race and ethnic relations (Amir, 1976; Miller & Brewer, 1984; Rossell & Hawley, 1983; St. John, 1975; Stephan & Feagin, 1980). Interracial contact (integration) is, in fact, one of the most researched topics in the social sciences. Unfortunately, the study of intergender contact has been neglected, but we can make some inferences from research on the conditions and effects of interracial contact.

For at least three decades, intergroup contact has been a mudsill of the entire effort of racial desegregation.[1] The "contact hypothesis" assumes that intergroup animosities exist partly because of stereotyped expectations and misperceptions of other people's beliefs, attitudes, and intentions (Jones, 1972, p. 43). The goals of contact are to reduce negative and ill-founded attitudes toward outgroups by fostering realistic attitudes (presumably positive) through face-to-face contact. Insofar as intergroup hostilities derive from social distance resulting from segregation, contact should diminish invidious categorizations and inculcate positive attitudes. The principal basis of contact theory is drawn largely from cognitive social psychology (Allport, 1958; Tajfel, 1969).

The contact hypothesis supposes that "prejudice (unless deeply rooted in the character structure of the individual) may be reduced by equal-status contact between majority and minority groups in the pursuit of common goals" (Allport, 1958, p. 267). Besides the idea of equal status, explanatory conditions associated with the contact hypothesis include the opportunity for contact (such as frequency, duration, and location); cooperative versus competitive goals; the existence of superordinate goals; the degree of interpersonal intimacy; the extent of institutional support; the direction and intensity of initial attitudes; the racial/ethnic balance; the existence of shared beliefs and interests; and forced versus voluntary contact (see Amir, 1976, for a thorough review). Researchers have assumed that positive effects vary with the extent to which some or all of these favorable conditions are met. They have often assumed, quite wrongly, that many of these conditions can be effectively constructed.

Over the past 30 years, numerous studies have found negative results in desegregated settings in the form of increased isolation, prejudice, hostility, and/or loss of self-esteem for minorities. Some have found no changes whatsoever. To be sure, others have reported favorable results, such as reduced prejudice and/or the lessening of interracial hostility (for reviews, see Amir, 1976; Carithers, 1970; McClendon, 1974; Pettigrew, 1971; St. John, 1975; Simpson & Yinger, 1985). At this point, however, the contact hypothesis remains largely unsupported, and the effect of intergroup contact on stereotypes is thus problematic.[2]

Much depends on the conditions of the contact situation. Some conditions, such as institutional support, duration of contact, and the existence of cooperative experiences, can be adjusted and made optimal by appropriate program planning and design. The condition of equal status may, however, be difficult to implement. Although definitions of equal status vary, the issue boils down to this: Does equal status *apply only* to the immediate contact situation or does it *apply also* to the status people bring with them to the situation? According to Cohen and Roper (1972):

> The oft made assumption that one has only to join blacks and whites on an officially "equal" footing in the same building for "equal status" relations to develop is not sound. . . . Belief systems concerning race and other status characteristics are so powerful that they will likely reinforce rather than damage stereotypical beliefs. (pp. 645, 657)

In an extensive review of the equal-status concept, I drew a similar conclusion (Riordan, 1978).

Far less is known about the effects of gender integration. One might reasonably assume, however, that the contact hypothesis would apply to gender in much the same way as it does to race. Consequently, the matter of equal status would be pivotal. Does sex, like race, function as a diffuse-status characteristic? The answer appears to be yes.

According to Lockheed and Klein (1985), "research on unstructured cross-sex interaction indicates that it is characterized by a lack of cooperation and male dominance" (p. 199). This appears to hold true for both children and adults. Numerous studies show that males are more likely to assume leadership positions, to be more verbally active, and to be more influential than females in all types of groups and situations (see Lockheed, 1985; Lockheed & Klein, 1985; Meeker & Weitzel-O'Neill, 1977; for studies showing contradictory results, see Eagly, 1978; Riordan, 1983; Webb, 1982). Lockheed and Klein (1985) state:

Evidence shows that as early as the elementary school years, sex as a status characteristic can be detected in children's cross-sex behavior and attitudes. . . . By the senior high school level, male domination of mixed-sex groups is well documented. (p. 192)

Thus, mixed-sex interaction appears decidedly unequal. Not surprisingly, gender stereotypes seem relatively unchanged as a result of contact (Broverman et al., 1972; Nash, 1975; Stein & Smithells, 1969; Williams, Bennett, & Best, 1975). On the other hand, an ideally conditioned coeducational school may shift the effects of cross-sex contact. Such circumstances could be created through some form of intervention treatment (Lockheed & Hall, 1976; Lockheed, Harris, & Nemceff, 1983; Pugh & Wahrman, 1983).

Currently, however, mixed-sex interaction in school or elsewhere is rare. Herein lies a paradox of coeducation: A setting that is supposedly integrated is, in fact, sex segregated. Classroom observations of student interaction consistently show that same-sex interchanges account for most peer group interaction in preschool, elementary, and junior high school settings (see Lockheed & Klein, 1985 for a review of studies). A review of educational prospects for women in higher education concludes that mixed-sex classroom interaction may be negative for women (Hall & Sandler, 1982). That study finds that women are likely to be ignored by male classmates, have their contributions discounted, and be subjected to stereotyped language and expectations. A more recent report reveals that the negative effects are even more severe, taking the form of sexual harassment and physical threat (Hughes & Sandler, 1988).

Lockheed (1985) reports disappointing results from a school intervention project aimed at increasing cross-sex interaction. Before the beginning of the school year, teachers of fourth- and fifth-grade classrooms participated in a two-day workshop that provided examples of and demonstrated methods for promoting cross-sex interaction. The classrooms of these teachers became the experimental group and were compared with a group of classrooms where teachers had not received the intervention treatment. Data on cross- and same-sex interactions, gender work-partner preferences, and sociometric ratings of actual classmates were obtained at both the beginning and end of the school year. The study found more cross-sex interaction in the experimental classrooms (44 percent compared with 37 percent for the control group) and an attitudinal increase among boys (but not girls) for working in mixed-sex groups generally. With regard to the actual preferences for working with their classmates (the clique structure of the classroom), however, Lockheed notes the "remarkable stability" of the preference for same-sex classmates in both experimental and control classrooms. Lockheed concludes that the intervention program failed to change the sociometric structure of the classroom. Student preferences for same-sex work patterns in the classroom remained unchanged despite the increase in cross-sex interaction. Understandably, Lockheed identifies sex segregation in coeducational schools as "The Issue of the Eighties" (1985), having noted elsewhere that it is the norm rather than the exception (1976).

Egalitarian Sex-Role Development

A fourth case for coeducation concerns preparing young people for less differentiated gender roles. Until fairly recently, single-sex schooling was not at odds with the world beyond the classroom. Boys were encouraged and expected to follow their fathers' activities; likewise, girls would follow their mothers'. Moreover, adult sex roles were segregated in the home, on the job, and in leisure activities. Outside of school, children largely engaged in sex-segregated activities. In that cultural context, sex-segregated schooling made normative sense.

Today, however, men's and women's roles have become less differentiated. Traditional sex roles, that is, a family where the father works and the mother and one or more children are at home, no longer characterize the American family. In the United States, the two-wage-earner family is the most common form (54 percent of couples with children both work), and nearly one-fourth of all children 17 or under live with only one parent (Hacker, 1983). Comparable trends exists in England (Halsey, 1972). Increasingly, then, men and women share domestic chores, occupations, and leisure, creating a greater discontinuity between sex-segregated schooling and life in the larger community.

To meet these changing conditions, adults need skills and traits associated with both masculine and feminine sex-role stereotypes. Coeducation may provide this cross-sex role learning in two ways. First, daily mixed-sex interaction may give students the opportunity to observe opposite-sex role behavior and to develop appropriate expectations. As noted above, however, coeducational schools are generally sex-segregated. Second, curricula in sex-fair schools should expose students to materials and situations that portray nonstereotyped roles for both males and females. In sex-biased schools or classrooms, though, students may learn sex-stereotyped roles. For example, if males are continually rewarded for dominant behavior and scientific careers while females receive reinforcement for passive behavior and nonscientific careers, traditional roles and expectations are learned.

Equality of Educational Opportunity

Recent history has found women more enthusiastic about coeducation than men. Understandably, many women regard it as a means of securing their natural and civil rights. Having been entirely excluded from schooling for centuries and then excluded from male schools, feminists have, until now at least, considered coeducation the *sine qua non* on the road to complete equity between the sexes. Indeed, today single-sex schooling violates, in spirit, the Educational Amendments of 1972. Title IX of these amendments states: "No person in the United States shall, on the basis of sex, be excluded from participation in, be denied the benefits of, or be subjected to discrimination under any education program or activity receiving Federal financial assistance" (Educational Amendments of 1972, Sec. 901, a). Although Title IX does not mandate how educational equity is to be achieved, it does indicate that educational programs in coeducational schools may not be segregated by sex. Thus, Title IX provides legal support for coeducation as the appropriate mode of schooling.

Title IX is clearly the broadest and most comprehensive of the sex discrimination laws applicable to schools. Title IX prohibits sex discrimination in admissions and student treatment within schools. With regard to admissions, however, Title IX is limited to vocational, professional, and graduate schools, and to public undergraduate schools, except those that have been traditionally and continuously open to only one sex. Thus, the admissions regulations of Title IX do not apply to preschools, elementary and secondary schools, or public undergraduate schools that have historically been single-sex institutions.[3]

Title IX does require all schools receiving federal financial assistance to treat all students, once admitted, without discrimination on the basis of sex. Thus, boys and girls must be provided equal treatment with regard to

1. Participation in all courses offered and all extracurricular activities
2. Participation in benefits, services, and financial aid
3. The use of school facilities

Therefore, mixed-sex schools may not, by law, differentially allocate courses or curricula, discriminate in career or academic counseling, or segregate boys and girls in the use of school facilities. Yet many policies of Title IX are virtually impossible to monitor and/or enforce in coeducational schools. Even when courses are technically open to both sexes, a violation of Title IX occurs if members of either sex are discouraged from enrolling in a particular course by either formal or informal counseling. Demonstrating such discouragement, however, is a formidable undertaking.

On the face of things, single-sex schools differentiate according to sex. Yet single-sex schools do guarantee equality of treatment within school, with or without Title IX. Moreover, Feldblum, Krent and Watkins (1986, p. 173) point out that all-female organizations may "counteract the societal disadvantages that women have suffered," thus aiding women to ultimately achieve equality with men. These authors probe the legal doctrines under which single-sex organizations might be defended in the face of legal challenges based upon Title IX and state ERA statutes. They argue the case for employing the "compensatory purpose doctrine"

> in situations where acting in a sex-blind or "equal" manner would result in perpetuating existing inequalities. A female single-sex organization meets this standard if it helps rectify the harmful effects of living in a society in which girls and boys, women and men, are neither perceived as equals nor treated equally in mixed-sex setting[s]. (Feldblum et al., 1986, p. 173)

The key questions are whether girls or boys are denied equal educational benefits by virtue of segregation and whether coeducation is better able to guarantee that neither sex will be so denied.

Significantly, the Title IX legislation was *not* based on data specifically demonstrating inequities and/or discrimination in single-sex schools. The law was based largely on discrimination in access to facilities and resources within the context of coeducation. The issue and problems of what to do about single-sex schools were actually an afterthought (Congressional Quarterly Almanac, 1971; Fishel & Pottker, 1977a, Chapter 5). The supportive data largely came from instances of sex discrimination in coeducational institutions. Such instances included sex differentiation in facilities, athletic budgets, course and curriculum selection, pedagogical and counseling practices, teachers' expectations for students, and textbook content (Fishel & Pottker, 1977b). Hence, the legislation under Title IX was intended to eliminate sex discrimination in coeducational schools and classrooms.[4]

Conceivably, single-sex schools do not deny equal benefits to boys and girls. Rather, their facilities might be "separate but equal." That ploy helped to maintain racial segregation from 1896 to 1954 (see *Plessey* v. *Ferguson*, 1896), but is now generally discounted as a myth (*Brown* v. *Board of Education*, 1954; Orfield, 1976). Thomas Sowell (1976) has argued that black academic success seems to have been located, more often than not, in all-black schools. Among high-achieving blacks, Sowell notes that Thurgood Marshall, Martin Luther King, Jr., Edward Brooke, and Jesse Jackson graduated from all-black schools. Nonetheless, only scant evidence exists about how public single-sex schools might provide a separate education for males and females without denying equal benefits to both sexes.[5] In any case, coeducation does not necessarily guarantee equal benefit.

The most extensive study regarding the academic effects of mixed- and single-sex schooling was conducted by the International Association for the Evaluation of Educational Achievement (IEA). This project began in the mid-1960s with a study of mathematical ability, and extended from 1966 to 1973 to include six other school subjects in 21 countries. Identical tests and questionnaires were developed and translated into several languages. In all, 133,000 students, 13,500 teachers, and 5,450 schools were involved in this study. Although the issue of mixed and single-sex schools was not central to the design of the study, information regarding school type was available and used in a number of IEA reports.

For this IEA data base, students in single-sex secondary schools scored higher, in general, in mathematics achievement than did their counterparts in coeducational schools (Husen, 1967). The IEA study of science also revealed positive effects among students attending single-sex schools. While the male/female differences in science were smaller in coeducational schools among 10- to 11-year-old students, this did not hold true for secondary school students who were in their terminal year. Among students 14 to 18 years of age, the difference in science performance between boys and girls was greater in coeducational schools (see Comber & Keeves, 1973: Table 6.19, p. 152). The male/female difference in achievement almost invariably increased, the longer students were in school. In 11 of 15 countries, the male/female gap in science widened more in coeducational than in single-sex schools (see also Kelly, 1978).

In a recent re-analysis of these data concentrating on schools in the United States and England only, Finn (1980) found that students in single-sex schools outperformed students in mixed-sex schools in tests of reading comprehension, word knowledge, biology, chemistry, and physics. Taken as a whole, these reports offer considerable support in favor of single-sex schools, despite the fact that the IEA study allowed for only a limited control for selection factors. Across a variety of cultures, school types and curricula, the academic achievement of students in single-sex schools was higher than that of students in mixed-sex schools.

Over the past decade, IEA conducted a second international survey of mathematics and science. During the past several years, early reports of the second IEA study have begun to appear and suggest even stronger single-sex school effects, especially among females, in less-developed countries such as Thailand, Nigeria, and Swaziland (see Jimenez & Lockheed, 1989; Lee & Lockheed, 1989; Lockheed & Komenan, 1988). These recent studies are discussed again in Chapter 7. Thus, the empirical evidence does not lend support to the argument that coeducation provides greater equality of academic achievement across gender. Of course, equality of educational opportunity is a broader concept and not necessarily equated with a narrow and standardized measure of academic achievement.

THE CASE FOR SINGLE–SEX SCHOOLING

Role Models

Role modeling is a developmental process whereby individuals with certain attributes, such as race, sex, and class, identify with other individuals having similar attributes and pattern their behavior after that of the models. Psychological behaviorism provides that people

> learn by observing both the activities of others (the models) and the consequences of these actions. Later on, in similar circumstances, an individual is likely to "try out" the behavior he has observed *if* it was reinforced for the model. . . . However, whether or not an individual will continue to behave thus depends on whether or not he is rewarded. Modeling, in short, informs a person of a new activity and its likely consequences, but whether it becomes part of his repertoire depends on his own experiences. (Kunkel & Nagasawa, 1973, p. 534)

The first case for single-sex schooling is that it provides boys and girls more successful role models of their own sex.[6] Teachers, counselors, and classmates model sex-appropriate behavior for all students from the earliest school years. Single-sex schools may be particularly advantageous for girls, since the top students in all subjects will be females capable of serving as successful role models. In addition, the teachers in girls' schools are predominantly women.

To a somewhat lesser extent, the same reasoning applies to boys' schools. More successful academic role models of the same sex are available, lending greater legitimacy to being a good student. It is important to note, however, that the percentage of male teachers in all-boys schools may be significantly lower than the percentage of female teachers in all-girls schools. Finn (1980, Table II) reports that in America, 63 percent of the teachers at boys' schools are men, compared with 93 percent women teachers in girls' schools. In England, the staff at boys' schools is 77 percent male; at girls' schools, 87 percent female. In American coeducational secondary schools the teaching staff is about 50 percent male, whereas in public elementary schools, over 80 percent of the teachers are female (see Figure 3.1).

Coed schools not only offer fewer role models but also differentiate student roles according to sex. Shaw (1980) argues that "mixed schools are essentially boys' schools in so far as they are dominated by boys' interest" (p. 73). To the extent that this is so, there will be less difference for boys between the two types of schools. In single-sex female schools, however, girls must necessarily compete and achieve in all positions, including some that might otherwise be considered "masculine."

Some research on the effects of role models in school shows that girls consistently demonstrate academic superiority over boys in American elementary schools, but that they lose this advantage in secondary schools. Historically, American elementary schools have had a predominance of female teachers, who have served as role models for female students. Until recently, the Armed Services constituted the largest male educational system in the United States. Studies show that the Army has been unusually successful in basic academic skills training, even with previously very low-achieving men (Sexton, 1969).

Tidball (1980) conducted an analysis of 1116 women's college graduates who were randomly selected from three editions of *Who's Who of American Women*. For each of the 348 colleges (coed and single sex) attended by these women, Tidball plotted the relationship between the number of women achievers and the number of women faculty at the college. She obtained an extremely high correlation ($r = .96$). "This is not to say that an abundance of adult women role models is the only predictor of subsequent achievement by women students; but it does reinforce the relative importance of the relationship in comparison with other institutional variables" (p. 508).

An interesting twist on this theme comes from a 1973 study of second-, fourth-, and sixth-grade students in Canada, the United States, England, and Nigeria (Johnson, 1973). Although American and Canadian girls exceeded boys in several reading areas, the pattern was reversed in England and Nigeria, where, in contrast to most of the rest of the world, there are significant numbers of male elementary school and reading teachers. Boys' reading scores also significantly exceed those of girls in Germany, where most elementary teachers are also male (Downing, 1973; Dwyer, 1973). A more recent study (Klainin & Fensham, 1986)

FIGURE 3.1. Men Teachers as a Percent of All Classroom Teachers in Public Elementary and Secondary Schools in the United States, 1947-1978

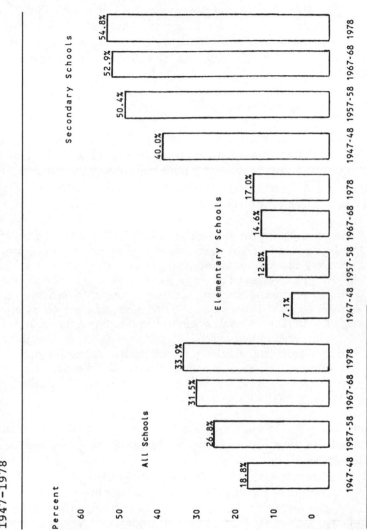

Source: Grant and Eiden (1981, p. 57).

in Thailand reports that girls score higher than their boy counterparts in physical science knowledge and attitudes toward the subject. The finding is contrary to the worldwide problem of girls' underachievement in science. The authors note that the majority of science teachers in Thailand are female and offer this as a likely explanation. Such findings support the importance of same-sex role models, which occurs most often in single-sex schools and/or classrooms (see also Hamilton, 1985; Vockell & Lobonc, 1981).

Traditional Sex-Role Development

Historically, a central function of both single-sex and coed schools has been the development of appropriate sex roles. As part of their surrogate parent function, schools have had some responsibility for promoting "proper" gender identities among students. Hyde (1971) describes how single-sex and coed advocates differ on this point.

> The essential principle of single-sex education has been the belief that boys and girls should define themselves as men and women by undergoing education or training appropriate to their different needs, obligations, and expectations and that this education is best conducted by teachers of the same sex, seen as models of manliness or womanhood, in a school community dominated by the values of a single sex. . . . The essential principle of coeducation is the belief that since "life is coeducational," boys and girls should go to school together so as to grow continuously in mutual understanding and respect. The coeducational school has thus been seen as an enlarged family rather than as . . . an institution in which the young are indoctrinated in the lore or "mysteries" of one sex. (p. 20)

Schools thus offer lessons about how to act as males and females. Single-sex schools are more likely to promote traditional sex roles emphasizing the distinctive characteristics of each sex. Coed schools, on the other hand, tend to teach egalitarian sex roles both in theory (vis-à-vis Title IX) and in practice (coed teacher role models, at least in secondary schools).

Coeducation serves the traditional masculine and feminine needs of students less effectively. Typically, the needs and interests of one sex are subordinated to those of the other. Kolesnik (1969) hypothesizes that coeducation may contribute "to the convergence of sex roles in modern society and the consequent confusion among men as well as women as to what masculinity and femininity are all about" (p. 10). To whatever extent he or she serves as a role model for students, no teacher, of whatever sex, can be both a masculine and feminine role model.

Boys, like girls, need adult approval from someone they respect and admire, someone with whom they identify. In many elementary schools boys find no such person. Likewise, in secondary schools girls are short-changed by a scarcity of female teachers and a male-dominated curriculum. Lockheed (1976) concludes "that coeducation impacts negatively on boys in the early grades and negatively on girls in the later grades and in secondary school" (p. 7).

Sex Differences in Curriculum Opportunities

A third case for single-sex schooling is that it provides uncon-strained access to the full range of educational curricula for all students. Historically, schools have provided different curricula for male and female students. Girls had and still have unequal access to education generally, which in effect excludes them entirely from the curriculum (Deble, 1980). But the opportunity to learn involves more than simply having access to the school.

In general, boys and girls have pursued different patterns of course work, even when their actual number of years of schooling has been the same. The question is whether such patterns are influenced by the mixed- or single-sex character of the school. Both single- and mixed-sex schools restrict some subjects to students of each sex (Shaw, 1976). Typically such restrictions apply among the vocational subjects and, to a lesser extent, among the sciences, math, and the humanities. Benn and Simon (1972) discovered that half of the 587 mixed-sex British schools they studied restricted some subjects to boys (engineering, gardening, woodwork, technical drawing, building, pottery, surveying) and other subjects to girls (needlework, clothes design, dancing, human biology). The most typical reason offered was that teachers of boys' subjects refused to include girls in their classes!

Sex differences in curriculum allocations also arise when one sex or the other is discouraged from enrolling in particular courses. Through-out the world, boys are channeled into mathematics and science more actively, while girls are directed toward courses in languages and the humanities. To some extent, of course, these routings are based upon cultural values of the home and society and reflect existing career op-portunities. At the same time, school practices reinforce and perpetuate these cultural attitudes. Except for boys' schools that are academic and girls' schools that are entirely or primarily vocational, single-sex schools are better able to overcome this bias. In comprehensive schools offering both academic and vocational subjects, however, covert channeling of girls into vocational or nonscientific courses would occur less often in single-sex schools.

In most schools, course selection and advisement is the function of guidance counselors. Both male and female counselors often hold a negative bias toward females considering nontraditional occupations (Fox, 1977; Oliver, 1975). Sex bias in counseling is very subtle and most often unintentional. Pietrofesa and Schlossberg (1977) found that male counselors were less directive with women than were female counselors, perhaps reflecting less concern with the consequences of their decisions. Bingham and House (1977) report similar results from a survey of high school counselors. Men agreed more often than women that (1) all women's roles are secondary to motherhood and (2) training women for high-level jobs is wasteful. Thus, female counselors seem preferable to males for advising female students (see also Shafer, 1976; Thomas & Stewart, 1971). Presumably, single-sex schools for women would provide mostly female counselors. The positive effect of that may be inferred from college studies showing that women in all-female schools choose nontraditional majors and take mathematics and science courses more often than women at coeducational colleges (Astin & Panos, 1969; Carnegie Commission on Higher Education, 1973).

Teacher–Student Interaction in the Classroom

Another way of viewing exposure to schooling is to consider the time in school that students actually spend in learning activities. Finn, Reis, and Dulberg (1980) label this *engaged time,* differentiating it from *allocated time.* Whereas allocated time is the amount of course work provided, engaged time is the amount of teaching and learning that go on in classrooms. Sex differences in engaged time may be common. Blackstone (1976) suggests that the differences in boys' and girls' performance in primary schools derives, at least partly, from differences in teachers' expectations and behavior.

Many studies indicate that teacher–student interaction in the classroom differs systematically by sex. Seewald, Leinhart, and Engel (1977) observed that second-grade teachers made more academic contacts with girls in reading and more with boys in mathematics. Having noted no differences in initial abilities, the researchers found sex differences in end-of-year achievement scores. Significantly, they also reported that the teachers had actually spent the same amount of total time with boys and girls in both subjects—the difference was specifically in engaged academic time. Lockheed (1976) obtained similar results in a study of 90 second- and fifth-grade teachers.

> After the effects of student achievement, SES, race, and school mobility had been partialled out . . . teachers still held significantly higher

expectations for the reading achievement of girls over boys. . . . it was found [also] that teacher expectations were significantly related to actual student learning increase. (p. 5)

Palardy (1969) compared a group of first-grade teachers who believed boys could read as well as girls, with a second group who felt boys would be inferior readers. At the end of the academic year, Palardy found no differences between the reading scores of boys and girls in the first group, whereas he found large differences in favor of girls in the second group.

Numerous studies show that students tend to behave in accordance with their teachers' expectations (Rosenthal & Jacobson, 1968). Dwyer (1973) reviewed the research on sex stereotyping of reading and noted that it was viewed as a feminine activity. She concluded that male disinterest in reading was a consequence of reading's being stereotyped as incompatible with male sex-role standards. Not surprisingly, the more that reading is viewed as an appropriate task (as in all-boys schools), the better boys learn to read. The same process probably accounts for girls' relative lack of success in mathematics and science.

The expectations of secondary school teachers are not well researched. It appears, though, that the positive expectations that elementary school teachers have toward girls in reading either change or are balanced by similar expectations for secondary school boys. The change may be partly due to the more balanced sex ratio among teachers in most secondary schools. At any rate, by the end of high school and into college, teachers' expectations are biased in favor of males in most academic areas as well as in general educational encouragement (Brophy & Good, 1974; Good & Findley, 1982). At the college level, Hall and Sandler (1982) report that teachers in coeducational schools may devalue the work of female students relative to males and encourage men to solve class problems while simply solving the same problems for women, thereby promoting female helplessness.

In summary, boys may be disadvantaged in early grades, and girls in later grades by biased teacher expectations. On that basis, boys might fare better in single-sex elementary schools, and girls might fare better in single-sex secondary schools and colleges. In both cases, the effects of sex-biased teacher expectations might be mitigated.

Sex Stereotypes in Peer Interaction

Students interact not only with their teachers but also with other students. Student peer interaction occurs throughout the school day both in and out of the classroom, making up an estimated 29 percent of

a student's experiences in a typical classroom (Lockheed, 1982). Generally, cross-sex peer interaction in schools involves male dominance, male
leadership, sex stereotypes, and a lack of cooperation (Hall & Sandler,
1982; Hughes & Sandler, 1988; Lockheed & Klein, 1985). These studies
suggest, however, that cross-sex peer interaction is not common, even in
coeducational schools. Nonetheless, one can reasonably assume that the
aforementioned problems do not occur in single-sex schools.

In a series of task-oriented experiments, Lockheed and Hall (1976)
investigated the behavior of mixed-sex and all-female groups. As predicted by status characteristic theory, men dominated mixed-sex groups
when the subjects had had no previous experience with the task. However, mixed-sex groups composed of individuals who had first experienced the task in a single-sex condition displayed a pattern of equal-
status behavior between males and females. The implication is that
mixed-sex interaction generally invokes a process of status generalization where typical male–female stereotypes operate. Initial familiarity
with the task in a single-sex setting, on the other hand, appears to
deactivate or at least mitigate the process of status generalization. Casserly (1978) reports a similar finding from a review of special programs in
science and mathematics for girls; namely, the most successful programs
relied on older girls to counsel, encourage, and tutor younger ones initially in a single-sex setting. These reports lend particularly strong support to the value of single-sex schools for girls, at least as a short-term
alternative to coeducation in terms of eventually producing more equitable male–female interaction.

The Adolescent Subculture

In a book entitled *The Adolescent Society* (1961) James Coleman put
forth the idea that our society has created an adolescent subculture that
favors physical attractiveness and heterosexual popularity over academic
achievement, especially within the schools themselves. The adolescent
subculture undermines the attainment of educational goals.

> In the normal activities of a high school, the relations between boys
> and girls tend to increase the importance of physical attractiveness,
> cars and clothes, and to decrease the importance of achievement in
> school activities. . . . It is commonly assumed, both by educators and
> by laymen, that it is "better" for boys and girls to be in school together
> during adolescence, if not better for their academic performance,
> then at least better for their social development and adjustment. But
> this may not be so. . . . Co-education in some high schools may be
> inimical to *both* academic achievement *and* social adjustment. The

dichotomy often forced between "life adjustment" and "academic emphasis" is a false one, for it forgets that most of the teenager's energy is not directed toward either of these goals. Instead, the relevant dichotomy is cars and the cruel jungle of rating and dating versus school activities, whether of the academic or life adjustment [kind]. (pp. 50–51)

Powell and Powell (1983) claim that the adolescent subculture may have become the *raison d'être* of schooling proper, not merely an obstacle to education. They criticize the coeducationalist argument that mixed-sex schools are natural.

American adults and teenagers regard coeducational high schools as natural, normal, and inevitable. . . . The absence of boys in high school is unthinkable to most people precisely because the presence of boys and girls together is what high school is increasingly all about. (pp. 55–56)

What are the effects of the adolescent subculture on the academic and social-psychological outcomes of schooling? In a mixed-sex environment, girls may find it more difficult to compete academically, learning (perhaps subconsciously) that their success might be threatening to boys, who might then reject them as potential sexual partners (Blackstone, 1976). Shaw (1976) summarizes the dilemma.

The social structure of mixed schools may drive children to make even more sex-stereotyped subject choices, precisely because of the constant presence of the other sex and the pressure to maintain boundaries, distinctiveness, and identity. In all-girls' schools, being both clever and attractive is a compatible, but not necessary, combination. Such a combination may be less viable in a mixed school where, in a climate of overall anxiety about appropriate sex behavior, dichotomies are presented and choices have to be made. Little protection from, or alternatives to, failure (or success) in romantic competition are afforded. (p. 137)

It is not surprising to find that female college freshmen who attended a single-sex high school showed less (15.8 percent versus 40.9 percent) "fear of success" as measured by Horner's TAT instrument (Winchel, Fenner, & Shaver, 1974). The power of the adolescent subculture may be reduced in single-sex schools, where heterosexual distractions are fewer. This curtailment of the adolescent subculture might increase interest in academic affairs and enhance the disciplinary climate of the school.

Schneider and Coutts (1982) found the adolescent subculture more operative in mixed-sex than in single-sex Catholic schools (see also Trickett et al., 1982). They observed "major differences in the social-psychological environments of coeducational and single-sex high schools" (p. 904). A New Zealand study (Jones, Shallcrass, & Dennis, 1972) also confirms that the adolescent subculture is more likely to exist in mixed-sex than in single-sex schools. Both boys and girls in single-sex schools spent significantly more time on homework outside of school and were more likely to use an extra hour in school for study purposes than students in mixed-sex schools. Forty-six percent of the boys in the single-sex schools but only 39 percent of the coeducational boys wanted to be remembered as a brilliant student (other choices were "most popular student" and "leader in activities"). The difference was even greater for girls (41 versus 26 percent). The researchers also asked students, "What does it take to get to be important and looked up to by other students at school?" Students in single-sex schools were significantly more likely to identify being "a good scholar" than were students in coed schools, whereas students in coed schools were significantly more likely to identify "having a nice car" and "being in the leading crowd."

Order and Control

Schneider and Coutts (1982) found substantial support for the hypothesis that single-sex schools emphasize control and discipline more than mixed-sex schools. They found that females in single-sex schools perceived a greater emphasis on control and discipline than males in single-sex schools. In their analysis of American public and private schools Coleman, Hoffer, and Kilgore (1982) demonstrated the importance of discipline and order in accounting for cognitive outcomes generally.

What would account for the greater stress on control and order that is characteristic of female single-sex schools? One possible explanation is that women, like other subordinate groups, establish social relationships of "mechanical solidarity" involving greater emphasis on rules and external control (Durkheim, 1933/1965). Female teachers in both coeducational and single-sex schools are more likely than male teachers to encourage behaviors such as obedience, deference, and order. Male teachers, by contrast, are "more tolerant of such traits as restlessness and aggressiveness . . . [and] more inclined to grant students . . . autonomy and freedom from control" (Schneider & Coutts, 1982, p. 905). Assuming that the staff of all-female schools is predominantly female, and that discipline and order are critical factors in learning, one might predict that females (rather than males) in single-sex schools might profit most academically.

The issues of order and control in school disproportionately involve boys. Boys are usually the troublemakers, whether the school is mixed- or single-sex. Data from sophomores in Catholic high schools reveal that boys are more likely than girls to report themselves in trouble regardless of whether the school is mixed- or single-sex. Table 3.1 shows, however, that for both boys and girls the likelihood of being a disciplinary problem decreases considerably in single-sex schools. Hence, problems of order and control might be considerably reduced by a policy of single-sex schooling.

As noted earlier (both in this chapter and in Chapter 1), however, some proponents of mixed-sex schools have argued that this troublesome nature of boys can be reduced in a coeducational environment (Dale, 1971, 1974). In an American study, Jones and Thompson (1981) found that the classroom misconduct of boys was reduced by a policy of mixed-sex schooling. Critics of this view are quick to point out, however, that this benefit for boys is usually at the expense of girls (Arnot, 1983; Jones, Kyle, & Black, 1987; Sarah, Scott, & Spender, 1980; Shaw, 1980; Spender, 1982). Chapters 4, 5, and 7 will examine this question in more detail.

Religious Grounds

Finally, from a global perspective, coeducation is problematic for some religious groups, especially Muslims. The idea is at best disturbing and at worst repulsive. According to Delamont (1980):

TABLE 3.1. Percentage of Students Self-Reporting as Disciplinary Problems in Catholic Schools, 1980

Outcome Measure	Single-Sex Schools		Mixed-Sex Schools	
	Males	Females	Males	Females
Disciplinary Problem	13.9	8.8	20.9	12.7
Suspended or on Probation	9.5	2.8	13.1	6.0

Source: High School and Beyond, 1980 Sophomore Cohort, First Follow-Up (1982), National Center for Education Statistics, Washington, DC; see Chapter 5 of this volume for a description of the study.

There is considerable evidence that the various Muslim groups in Britain include many parents who do not approve of coeducation because it contradicts their principles of separate spheres for males and females. After puberty the respectable female should not be in the company of unrelated males, and so education becomes a problem. (p. 105)

In 1975, there were 400,000 Muslims in England, so their values would seem difficult to ignore. Worldwide, there are 400 million Muslims, most of whom are compelled by their religion to reject mixed-sex schools.

In the Republic of Ireland, religious constraints affect the gender context in schools for the majority Catholic population. The Catholic Church in Ireland has resisted coeducation. Historically, the Church has opposed dating, dancing, early marriage, and contraception. It is not surprising, therefore, that nearly 70 percent of the Catholic schools in Ireland are single-sex institutions (Hannon et al., 1983, p. 96).

Throughout the world, Hebrew day schools, which serve mostly an Orthodox Jewish community, have maintained a policy of single-sex schooling at the high school level. According to Rabbi Joseph Fisher (personal correspondence, 1988), "There are 151 boys-only schools, 96 girls-only, and 225 coed schools that are part of the Hebrew Day School system." Fisher (personal correspondence, 1986) summarizes the position of the National Society for Hebrew Day Schools in America.

The rule of law (*P'sak Halacha*) of our Great Rabbis (*Gedolai Hatorah*) is very clear . . . for bigger children there is a definite prohibition from the Torah for mixing boys and girls in the classroom. Younger children . . . may be permitted to be in a mixed class providing the situation is dire and the need is great in order to able to operate a school. . . . As recently as 1983 the Rabbinical Board of Torah Umesorah publicly reaffirmed the position of "Daas Torah" on this issue, to condemn the establishment of a coed high school in Milwaukee, Wisconsin [stating] "Therefore, do we the undersigned herewith proclaim and declare to any who would so err, co-education on a secondary level is prohibited by Torah law and Jewish tradition."

SUMMARY

The pros and cons of single- and mixed-sex schooling are complex. In some instances, the pros and cons are irrelevant, as is the case with Hasidic Jews, who insist on single-sex schooling based entirely on religious grounds. Considered carefully, this is *not* very different from the vast majority of schools in America, which began as mixed-sex schools on the basis of economic efficiency.

Mixed-sex schools are more economically efficient and provide a social environment in keeping with the modern world. Single-sex schools provide more successful role models for students and allow religious groups to maintain their traditional educational practices. Students in mixed-sex schools, both males and females, are likely to experience some sex bias from teachers, counselors, or fellow students. Sex bias in single-sex schools will be minimized. Single-sex schools display more order and control than mixed-sex schools. In all-boys schools, the greater control may be related to an increased need for order because of the higher incidence of disciplinary problems among boys, whereas in girls' schools, it may simply be traditional.

Single-sex schools promote traditional sex-role development. In theory, mixed-sex schools should provide greater opportunities for less traditional and more egalitarian sex-role learning. In practice, however, mixed-sex schools are typically sex segregated. Boys and girls still seem to prefer same-sex friends, and cross-sex interaction remains male dominated. Theoretically also, mixed-sex schools should mitigate or eliminate gender stereotyping, but the evidence for this is inconsistent at best. Mixed-sex schools provide equality of educational opportunity, de jure. Unfortunately, the law is limited and difficult to monitor. Beyond questions of admission, single-sex schools obviously do not discriminate by sex in providing educational opportunity.

Which type of school is more effective? Throughout this chapter, I have reviewed numerous studies of both cognitive and affective outcomes. Some of the studies are dated, though most are current. The quality of some studies is excellent, but most are below par, lacking controls for home background and other likely biasing factors. As noted in Chapter 1, there may be significant differences between the overall quality of boys' and girls' schools. By and large, however, the weight of the empirical evidence favors single-sex schools in terms of academic outcomes. Girls in single-sex schools, especially, seem to obtain higher cognitive outcomes than their counterparts in mixed-sex schools. This provides more than sufficient reason to more closely examine the social psychology of single-sex schools, which is the task of the next chapter.

The Formal and Informal Structure of the Schools

As with all institutions, schools operate within both a formal and informal structure. The values and norms associated with these structures govern most of what happens or does not happen in schools. Factors such as school size, physical facilities, faculty credentials, and faculty sex ratio, along with the established curriculum and corresponding course work, constitute the *formal* mechanics of the schools. Just as important, however, are the *informal* rules and the "hidden curriculum." The central forces that help form the informal norms are the socioeconomic backgrounds and the adolescent subculture (social values) of students in the school. This chapter examines the extent to which single- and mixed-sex schools differ in these formal and informal structures. The result is a description of the social psychological environment that distinguishes single- and mixed-sex schools.

We begin our factual analysis of this environment by examining the formal structure of single- and mixed-sex Catholic schools in the United States. To accomplish this, I use data from the High School and Beyond (HSB) survey of the high school class of 1982. HSB is a large nationwide study of 58,270 students in 1015 private, public, and church-related schools in the United States (see Chapter 5 for more detail on the sampling procedures). The HSB data contain a broad and highly specific set of both student and school information.

The HSB data are composed of two different samples. One is the regular school sample, which is representative of Catholic schools throughout the country. In addition, HSB drew a stratum of Catholic schools with a high proportion of either black or Hispanic students. These two samples differ in some important respects, especially with regard to the home background and racial characteristics of the students. In Chapter 5, therefore, I analyze and present results separately for each sample. In this chapter, however, I do not distinguish between the two samples, because the formal characteristics of the schools in both samples are similar.

THE FORMAL STRUCTURE OF THE SCHOOLS

The Physical Plant

Catholic high schools are generally small in comparison with public schools, regardless of gender context. Mixed-sex schools and single-sex girls' schools are especially small. Table 4.1 compares and displays several characteristics of the schools. Catholic all-boys schools enroll an average of about 800 students. These schools are considerably larger than either all-girls or coeducational schools, which average about 500 students in size.

Both boys' and girls' schools have higher tuition and per-pupil expenditures than do coeducational schools. The tuition at boys' schools ($1051) and per-pupil expenditure ($1482) are higher than at all-girls schools, where the average tuition is $973 and the per-pupil expenditure $1183. While the tuition at mixed-sex schools is low ($687), the per-pupil expenditure ($1023) is only a bit less than at girls' schools. Thus, single-sex boys' schools have greater financial resources to offer their students than do either coeducational facilities or single-sex girls' schools. Part of this "surplus" is due to the tuition at boys' schools. Part of it, however, must be due to some other form of "allocation" or "income," because the per-pupil expenditure in boys' schools is much higher than what would be expected from the difference in tuition. That is, boys in single-sex schools pay an average of only $78 more in tuition than do girls, whereas the schools spend an average of $299 more on boys.

Ironically, tuition at all-girls schools is higher than at mixed-sex schools by $286, but per-pupil expenditure is only $160 more (see Table 4.1). Somehow, the presence of boys in a school results in additional financial resources over and above tuition charges. This means that the money available for the education of girls in single-sex schools is more likely to come directly from family resources than from external sources, as must be the case in boys' and mixed-sex schools. Quite possibly, boys' schools and mixed-sex schools may generate additional income from sports and other social activities. Further on, we shall learn that girls in single-sex schools come from homes of lower socioeconomic means than girls in mixed-sex schools. Hence, there appears to be a double-barreled

TABLE 4.1. Formal Characteristics of Mixed- and
Single-Sex Catholic Schools in the United States[a]

	Boys' Schools	Mixed-Sex Schools[b]	Girls' Schools[b]
School Characteristic			
School Size	800	502	495
Annual Tuition (1980)	$1051	$687	$973
Per-Pupil Expenditure	$1482	$1023	$1183
Student/Faculty Ratio	20	18	17
% Students in College Program[c]			
Sophomore Year	.65	.54	.67
Senior Year	.74	.64	.68
Faculty Characteristics			
% Faculty with Advanced Degree	.61	.37	.43
% Faculty Female	.15	.56	.88
% Faculty at School 10 Years	.31	.15	.19
% High Faculty Commitment	.64	.55	.78
Number of Schools	22	33	29

[a] These data are based upon school record information completed by the
principal or other designated administrator of each school. The percentages
and means are weighted; the numbers of schools are unweighted.

[b] In their analysis of these same data, Lee and Bryk (1986) deleted eight
schools that contained a disproportionately high percentage of vocational
students. Five of these were girls' schools and three were coeducational.
They determined from a previous study that most of these schools specialized
in stenographic and clerical training. When these schools are eliminated,
the data in Table 4.1 change slightly on some of the characteristics.
Specifically, for girls' schools, school size = 491 and student/faculty
ratio = 16; for coeducational schools, school size = 616 and student/faculty
ratio = 20.

[c] These data are based upon student self-reports.

financial sacrifice for the girls attending single-sex schools and their
families. They receive less external financial support and have less socioeconomic home support.

   If financial resources of this nature were related to school outcomes, it would behoove girls to move to coeducational settings. It is
fairly well established, however, that the physical facilities of schools are
not significantly associated with academic success (Coleman et al., 1966;
Fuller, 1986; Mosteller & Moynihan, 1972). Nonetheless, it appears that
single-sex schools for girls do operate with a curious restriction of physi-

cal resources. Specifically, the ratio of tuition to per-pupil expenditure is higher in all-girls schools than in either boys' schools or coeducational institutions. This effectively means that students (and their families) in all-girls schools must bear a proportionally greater direct financial burden for their education than students in the other school types. In fact, girls attending these single-sex schools pay above-average tuition. If girls in single-sex schools are more successful than their counterparts in mixed-sex schools, as it turns out they are, it is not simply because the schools spend more money on their education. It is more likely to relate, in part, to the financial sacrifices that they endure and the strength of commitment that derives from these sacrifices. Concomitantly, all-girls schools may provide an academic atmosphere relatively free of nonacademic activities, such as highly competitive interscholastic sports.

One aspect of the physical plant that may advantage girls in single-sex schools is the student/faculty ratio. Table 4.1 shows that this ratio is smallest for students in all-girls schools and largest in all-boys schools. Comparing single- with mixed-sex schools for each sex separately, however, the differences are quite small. In their analysis of these data, however, Lee and Bryk (1986) deleted eight schools that contained a disproportionately high percentage of vocational students. Five of these were girls' schools and three were coeducational. When these schools are eliminated, the numbers for school size and class size change considerably. Specifically, for girls' schools, school size=491 and student/faculty ratio=16; for coeducational schools, school size=616 and student/faculty ratio=20. In any event, "evidence to date, from research and practice, does not generally support a policy of limiting class size in order to raise student achievement" (Tomlinson, 1988, p. 37). With regard to school size, however, Goodlad (1984) has argued in favor of smaller schools. I reconsider this in Chapter 7.

Another important structural characteristic of schools is the curriculum. Some schools provide essentially a vocational curriculum, while other schools offer mostly a college preparatory program. One of the most intriguing findings of the Coleman, Hoffer, and Kilgore (1982) report on Catholic and public schooling is that students in Catholic schools are far more likely to be placed in a college track than students in public schools, even after controlling for initial student ability. They argue that this reflects a school policy which positively impacts directly on students over and above student background and ability. There is disagreement as to whether or not the distribution of students in the curriculum is a function of school policy, student choice, or "bias" resulting from the self-selection of good schools by good students (Alexander & Pallas, 1983; Bryk, 1981; Coleman, Hoffer, & Kilgore, 1981; Goldberger & Cain, 1982; Kilgore, 1983). Whatever its source, the distribution of students in the various curricula is a school characteristic. Are there any differences regarding curriculum policy among single- and mixed-sex schools?

Table 4.1 indicates that during the sophomore year 65 percent of the students in boys' schools are enrolled in an academic program, compared with 54 percent in mixed-sex schools and 67 percent in girls' schools. By senior year, this figure has increased to 74 percent in boys' schools, 64 percent in mixed-sex schools, and 68 percent in all-girls schools. In an earlier analysis using data from the high school class of 1972, I found the same differences in curriculum enrollments between mixed- and single-sex schools (Riordan, 1985). It is apparent that coeducational institutions are somewhat less academic in their formal curriculum structure than are single-sex schools. This is confirmed as we look now at the faculty characteristics of these schools.

Characteristics of the Faculty

The credentials of the faculty have long been viewed as a critical factor in determining student outcomes. This is true despite the fact that research had consistently failed to confirm this belief (Coleman et al., 1966; Fuller, 1986). One way to measure these credentials is to examine the percentage of teachers in a school holding advanced degrees. Comparing all-girls schools with mixed-sex schools, Table 4.1 shows only a small difference in faculty educational training, favoring single-sex schools. The faculty of all-boys schools, however, is substantially better educated than the faculty of either of the other two school types.

Another widely held view is that students do better academically in the presence of same-sex role models. This theory was reviewed at length in Chapter 3. Needless to say, the faculty of all-girls schools is mostly female, whereas the reverse is true in all-male schools, as shown in Table 4.1. Coeducational schools are nearly proportional according to sex. In subsequent chapters, I will point often to this role-modeling effect.

Finally, we should take note of the sense of teacher morale and satisfaction in the schools. This characteristic can be demonstrated in several ways. The HSB survey asked administrators of the schools to evaluate teacher commitment and motivation. In addition, data were obtained regarding faculty turnover. As shown in Table 4.1, administrators report that teachers in girls' single-sex schools have the highest degree of commitment and motivation, followed by the teachers in boys' single-sex schools. This translates into a considerably large difference if we compare single-sex girls' with mixed-sex schools. In mixed-sex schools, only half the faculty display high commitment, whereas in all-girls schools, three-quarters of the faculty do so. This disparity in teacher motivation parallels the differences noted above in the structure of the academic curriculum and in faculty credentials. Finally, and not surprisingly, we can see from Table 4.1 that there is less teacher turnover in single-sex schools, especially boys' schools. All in all, single-sex schools seem to possess a more favorable formal academic environment than do mixed-sex schools.

THE INFORMAL ENVIRONMENT OF THE SCHOOLS

Socioeconomic Background of Students

In the HSB study, socioeconomic status is measured as a composite of five equally weighted standardized components: family yearly income, father's education, mother's education, father's occupational prestige level, and the possession of eight household items. The measure has a mean score of zero for both public and private students in the entire sample; for Catholic school students the overall mean is 0.31. The HSB survey is actually composed of two separate samples: a regular, mostly white sample and a special, mostly minority sample. These are described in detail in Chapter 5. In the regular sample, which is more typical, the socioeconomic status mean is .32, whereas it is only .10 in the specially drawn minority sample.

Table 4.2 shows the socioeconomic composition of mixed- and single-sex Catholic schools. It also provides specific estimates of total family income. In the discussion below and throughout the analysis, however, I rely on the composite measure of socioeconomic status. Throughout Table 4.2 (and in Table 4.3), I report the results for students in mixed-sex schools separately by sex. Unlike the formal characteristics of the school, student background characteristics and student attitudes and behaviors often differ according to sex, and often operate in the aggregate in sex-segregated ways. Moreover, in the analyses of outcomes presented in Chapters 5 and 6, I will report the influence of school type separately for males and females.

Table 4.2 reveals that the socioeconomic status of boys in Catholic schools is always higher than that of girls, regardless of school type. Yet the difference is significant only for students in single-sex schools. The male–female difference in single-sex schools is 0.20; in mixed-sex

TABLE 4.2. Home Background Characteristics of Students
in Mixed- and Single-Sex Catholic Schools
in the United States[a]

	Males		Females	
Characteristic	Single	Mixed	Single	Mixed
% Family Income > $25,000	.75	.66	.63	.65
Socioeconomic Status[b]	.42	.33	.22	.29
% Mother and Father in Home	.86	.81	.82	.80
% Four or > Children in Home	.45	.58	.47	.55
% Mother Worked-High School	.74	.66	.72	.64
% Mother Worked-Elementary	.59	.57	.65	.55
% Mother Worked-PreSchool	.37	.43	.33	.36
% High Parental Involvement in School[c]	.26	.31	.27	.25
Number of Students	605-669	404-483	754-881	468-535

[a] Percentages are based on a weighted sample of Catholic schools and represent
population estimates. Numbers of students are unweighted and differ slightly
according to each variable.

[b] A composite of five equally weighted standardized components: family yearly
income, father's education, mother's education, father's occupation (using
Duncan's occupational status scale), and eight household items. The overall
public and Catholic school mean together is zero. The Catholic school mean
is .31.

[c] This is a three-variable composite of parental participation in PTA,
parent-teacher conferences, and special school projects.

schools it is 0.04. These data are generally consistent with results from the
National Longitudinal Study of the High School Class of 1972 (Riordan,
1985; see also Lee & Bryk, 1986). The socioeconomic status of boys in
Catholic schools, especially single-sex schools, is clearly higher than that of
girls. In fact, it is higher than that of boys attending mixed-sex schools.

Boys in Catholic single-sex schools are a fairly selective group, in
contrast to girls. This finding is opposite to what one might expect. The
difference does not reflect simply traditional sex-role differentiation,

that is, that parents are willing to spend more money on the education of boys than girls. Instead, Table 4.2 indicates a greater economic sacrifice for the parents of girls in Catholic single-sex schools, because these families have only average socioeconomic status.

Parents who make the greatest economic sacrifice are more likely to select a single-sex school for girls; Table 4.2 shows that girls in single-sex schools come from homes with the lowest socioeconomic status on average. As noted earlier, tuition at all-girls schools is higher than at coeducational schools, so this economic sacrifice is even more salient. Parents of boys in Catholic schools, on the other hand, make a far smaller economic sacrifice. Technically, this amounts to a sex-by-school-type interaction. The socioeconomic status of boys in single-sex schools is equal to or greater than that of boys in mixed-sex schools. (In the special minority sample, the socioeconomic status of males is actually equal for the two school types; see Table 5.1.) Girls in single-sex schools, however, are always lower in socioeconomic status than girls in mixed-sex schools. Conceivably, the difference may be due to a greater parental concern for the fate (safety as well as academic progress) of girls in mixed-sex schools. Parents of low to average socioeconomic status may reason that boys will survive or even flourish in mixed-sex schools, but that the road is tough for girls. If so, they have an intuitive sense for the outcomes presented in Chapter 5, and the policy interpretations in Chapter 7.

Thus, girls in single-sex Catholic schools come from rather average homes compared with their counterparts in mixed-sex schools. Consequently, they are likely to have lower initial academic ability and less intellectual support in the home. On the other hand, it is possible that their commitment and motivation are higher because of the financial sacrifice made by their parents, which is intensified by the higher tuition in single-sex schools.

In any case, this male–female socioeconomic difference raises the issue of "selection bias." Analyses of the effects of schools must always contend with the potentially confounding influences of the home. In studies of this sort, observed differences between schools may possibly be due to differences in the home backgrounds of students. Typically, high performance is associated with both higher socioeconomic background and a hypothesized more effective school. This possibility looms large among boys in the regular sample and girls in the minority sample, where varying school outcomes might be attributed to the differences in socioeconomic status. This difference shapes the analysis of outcomes presented in Chapter 5.

Parental Presence in the Home, and Family Size

Beyond the socioeconomic and racial characteristics of students, the structure of the family is an important factor in the academic success of students (see Boocock, 1980, Chapter 4, for a review). Some evidence (Milne, Myers, Ginsburg, & Rosenthal, 1986) suggests that students from two-parent homes are more successful in school than students from single-parent households. In their national study of elementary and high school children, Milne et al. (1986) conclude:

> In general, students from two-parent families have higher scores on reading and math achievement tests than students from one-parent families. This is true for white and black students in elementary and high school.... The negative effects on achievement of living in a one-parent family are almost entirely mediated by other variables, particularly by income. (p. 131)

Although the evidence is not conclusive, the loss of a parent, either through work or a divorce, may be disadvantageous to academic progress.

To what degree do students in Catholic single- and mixed-sex schools differ regarding parental presence in the home? Table 4.2 displays the percentage of students in each school type with two parents present in the home, together with data regarding family size and working patterns of the mothers of students. There is virtually no difference in the number of parents in the home across either sex or school type. The only small exception is boys in single-sex schools, where 86 percent have two parents at home. Although not shown in Table 4.2, 83 percent of students in the regular sample have two parents at home, compared with only 71 percent in the minority sample. The average for students in public schools is 70 percent.

Another component of family structure is size. On average, students from smaller families (fewer children) are more successful in school than students from larger families (Steelman & Mercy, 1980; Zajonc, 1976). Conceivably, however, this may be a spurious effect due to the prior influence of social class. Table 4.2 also shows that students in single-sex schools come from smaller families than students in mixed-sex schools. In the case of males, this is probably related to their higher social class. For females, however, this represents an unusual pattern of low socioeconomic status and small family size. It may possibly contribute to the academic success of girls in single-sex schools.

The socioeconomic status of the home may temper or increase the effects of family size. Page and Grandon (1979) conclude that the effects of family size on ability are small after one adjusts for social class and ethnicity. Walberg and Marjoribanks (1976) found, however, that children from smaller families had higher cognitive ability, even after controlling for socioeconomic status. Generally, the research leans in the direction of an inverse relationship between family size and school achievement. Such a relationship suggests that parents with fewer children may be better able to provide the time, attention, and other resources conducive to an intellectually stimulating home climate than are parents with more children.

The Work Patterns of Mothers

The work patterns of mothers and their possible influence on the cognitive and affective development of children are controversial. As a result of both political and economic pressures, an increasing percentage of mothers find themselves in the work force. Generally, the research on maternal work status has failed to produce consistent results. One review (Heynes, 1982) notes that the school achievement outcomes of children of employed mothers differs very little from those of children of nonemployed mothers.

Some studies, in fact, report positive effects on student achievement among children of employed mothers in poor and/or minority households (Heynes, 1982; Milne et al., 1986; Woods, 1972). Other studies, however, indicate negative findings. Two studies in particular have found remarkably consistent results among dual-parent families. Milne et al. (1986) report a study of elementary school children showing significant negative effects of maternal employment on the school achievement of children from dual-parent families. This effect is primarily direct and unmediated by other variables in their model. These results were replicated among secondary school students (Milne et al., 1986). In both studies, the magnitude of the effect directly relates to the amount of time mothers work.

In traditional two-parent families where very low income is not a crucial issue, the loss of one parent's time as an educator is not offset by the added income. Presumably, parents may have positive effects on their children's achievement through educationally relevant activities in the home. Among low-income, single-parent homes (especially minority homes), however, Milne et al. (1986) confirmed the effect of parental employment to be positively related to achievement. The issue is obviously complex. The effects of family structure are often confounded with those of family size, birth order, and the distance between siblings.

Table 4.2 provides some interesting results regarding the employment patterns of mothers of students in the HSB Catholic school sample. The mothers of children in single-sex schools were *less* likely to have worked outside the home before the children entered elementary school than the mothers of children in mixed-sex schools. This small difference holds for both males and females, with the difference for males (6 percent) slightly higher than that for females (3 percent). This pattern seems predictable. Single-sex schools are traditional institutions patronized by traditional families, where a mother is likely to remain at home at least during the preschool years.

Surprisingly, however, the pattern changes during elementary school. During this period, mothers of students in single-sex schools, especially mothers of girls in single-sex schools, become more likely to work outside the home than mothers of students in mixed-sex schools. Mothers of girls in single-sex schools are 10 percent more likely to have been employed than mothers of girls in mixed-sex schools. The pattern is the same for mothers of boys, but the difference is only 2 percent. In high school, however, the pattern becomes fully consistent, with mothers of both girls and boys in single-sex schools 8 percent more likely to be working outside the home than mothers of both girls and boys in mixed-sex schools.

Thus, mothers of students in single-sex schools are more likely to remain at home during the preschool years. This traditional approach to early child development emphasizes the importance of a mother at home. Unexpectedly, however, during the school years, mothers of students in single-sex schools become nontraditional. They are more likely than mothers of students in mixed-sex schools to be employed. How can we account for this trend? One possibility, applicable especially to girls, is that mothers work in order to pay the tuition. As noted earlier, girls in single-sex schools come from homes of only average socioeconomic status. Conceivably, mothers may need to work to help with the costs of tuition. In the case of boys the socioeconomic hardship explanation is inappropriate, because boys in single-sex schools come from homes of above-average means. Possibly, as college approaches and mothers realize their sons are likely to go to college, the mothers of boys in single-sex schools enter the work force to help with anticipated college expenses.

Not shown in Table 4.2 is an important difference between the regular and minority school samples. Mothers in the minority sample are significantly more likely to have worked during all time periods than mothers in the regular sample, with very little variation across school type. This presumably reflects the large socioeconomic differences between the two samples.

Parental Involvement in the Schools

There is a growing literature on the importance of parental involvement for the success of students in school. It has been shown that parental involvement is directly related to both student and teacher performance in the classroom (Clark, 1983; Epstein, 1987; Rich, 1985). Although Catholic schools have been found to have greater parental involvement than public schools (Coleman & Hoffer, 1987), there appears to be little difference between single- and mixed-sex Catholic schools. Table 4.2 shows that parental involvement in the schools is low. Quite possibly, the extensive work patterns of mothers described above may account for the low parental involvement in the schools. In any event, there are no major differences on this variable that might favor single-sex schools.

Attitudes Toward Schooling

The attitudes that students bring from home to school affect their academic progress (Entwisle & Hayduk, 1982; Kahl, 1953). Once school begins, of course, these attitudes are a function of both the home and the school. Students with negative attitudes toward school are problematic learners. Unfortunately, measures of social psychological attitudes are more difficult to obtain than measures of socioeconomic status, race, or family structure. They are even more elusive in studies of schooling, because student attitudes are affected by both the school and the home.

Table 4.3 provides a measure of student attitudes expressed as the lowest level of schooling that a student would be satisfied with. Students in single-sex schools more commonly expect to graduate from college than students in mixed-sex schools. Among females, the gap between the two types is about 5 percent. Among males, however, 38 percent of the students in single-sex schools expect to finish college, compared with only 28 percent of the males in mixed-sex schools.

Although not shown in Table 4.3, most students expect to attend college, with very little difference across either sex or school type. Approximately 80 percent of the students in both school types expect to attend college. The only difference across school type occurs among males in the regular school sample—only 66 percent of males have college expectations in mixed-sex schools. For the most part, however, students in Catholic schools vary little in their general college expectations. Yet, with regard to specific attitudes toward college graduation, students in single-sex schools generally have higher expectations.

TABLE 4.3. Informal Characteristics of Mixed- and
Single-Sex Catholic Schools in the United States
(in percentages)[a]

Characteristic	Males		Females	
	Single	Mixed	Single	Mixed
Expect College Degree	.38	.28	.37	.32
Date Once/Week or More (Soph)	.40	.27	.35	.36
Date Once/Week or More (Sen)	.66	.60	.59	.58
3 Hours or More/Day TV (Soph)	.60	.54	.50	.50
3 Hours or More/Day TV (Sen)	.34	.30	.30	.28
15-35 Hours/Week Work (Soph)	.31	.29	.20	.16
15-35 Hours/Week Work (Sen)	.67	.62	.62	.59
5+ Hours/Week Homework (Soph)	.47	.31	.60	.45
5+ Hours/Week Homework (Sen)	.39	.32	.55	.46
Good Discipline in School[b]	.88	.85	.89	.85
Adolescent Subculture[c]	.59	.53	.51	.53
Number of Students	605– 669	404– 483	754– 881	468– 535

[a] Percentages are based on a weighted sample of Catholic schools and represent
population estimates. Numbers of students are unweighted and differ slightly
according to each variable.

[b] This is a six-variable composite containing the following items: students
regularly attend school, students generally do not cut classes, students
rarely talk back to teachers, students generally obey instructions, students
generally do not fight with each other, students never attack teachers. This
variable is aggregated to the school level. The figure shown here is the
average percentage in each school type reporting good discipline in the school.

[c] This is a composite measure of four variables aggregated to the school level.
Students were first selected from each school who identified themselves as
part of the "leading crowd." Then, among these students only, responses to
the following questions were aggregated and assigned to each school: how often
do you spend time going on dates; are you going steady with one person or
engaged; how do you feel toward good students; how do you feel toward athletic
students? (All questions were dichotomized.) Since this is an aggregated
school level variable, control for sex was not applied, although small
differences do exist across sex in mixed-sex schools. The figure shown here
is the average percent of leading crowd students in each school type engaging
in the combined activities.

As a whole, the college expectations of students in the minority sample slightly exceed the expectations of students in the regular, predominantly white sample. This lack of racial difference in general attitudes toward school has often been noted (Coleman et al., 1966; Gordon, 1972). Generally, researchers conclude that educational aspirations do not differ by race. Differences appear only when students attempt to translate their aspirations into reality.

Do these expectations reflect the influences of the home or the school? Attitudes toward school are probably shaped both at school and at home. Hence, the results may be spurious; that is, home background is a potential common cause of both school type and attitudes toward school. Figure 4.1 depicts this set of relationships.

A regression of expectations for college graduation upon both home background and school type allows estimates of the relative effects of each predictor variable. This amounts to examining the differences that would exist across school type if students in both single- and mixed-sex schools came from the same kinds of homes. I used a general multivariate analysis (MANOVA) in which the socioeconomic composite and the family variables in Table 4.2 were applied as factors and covariates.

The estimates provided by this procedure may be less precise than desirable, because the procedure involves a dichotomous dependent variable in a regression equation. Although this typically results in heteroscedasticity, it is not necessary at this point to go beyond the approximations that are present here. In the analysis of outcomes, these variables are treated as independent predictors, in which case their dichotomous nature is no longer problematic.

It turns out that home background does not change the influence of school type on student attitudes, although the overall effect of the home is three to four times as great as the effect of the school. Students in single- and mixed-sex schools differ with regard to the lowest level of

FIGURE 4.1. Modeling the Effects of Home and School
on Student Attitudes

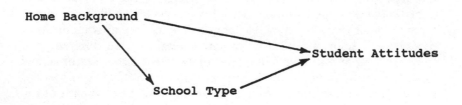

schooling they desire, and this difference persists even after the influence of home background has been taken into account.

Student Behavior Outside of School

Students in single- and mixed-sex schools may differ in their behavior outside of school. To that extent, differential cognitive and affective outcomes may derive from factors beyond the home or the school. Moreover, these activities will, in turn, influence the informal climate of the schools. If students in one school watch more television or are more likely to work part-time, for example, they may exhibit lower test scores in school. Table 4.3 summarizes the dating, working, and television-viewing patterns of students.

The dating behavior of students in Catholic schools is remarkably similar for boys and girls across the two school types in both samples. About 33 percent of the sophomores report dating at least as often as once a week; about 60 percent of the seniors date at least once a week (see Table 4.3). Very few differences emerge between mixed- and single-sex schools. The only exception is that boys in single-sex schools date more often than boys in mixed-sex schools. Although this difference is 13 percent in the sophomore year, it is only 6 percent by senior year. This difference, however, reflects a broader pattern: Boys' schools manifest a higher level of adolescent subculture norms than in any other school type, as will be discussed shortly.

Table 4.3 also concerns television viewing. During the sophomore year, better than half of the Catholic school students watch more than three hours of TV per day. In most instances, boys watch more than girls, but the differences are small. Across types of school, no substantial differences are discernible in either the sophomore or senior years. During the senior year, television viewing drops by nearly half. About one-third of the students watch more than three hours per day. This reduction probably reflects increased dating as well as increased employment, from sophomore to senior years.

During the sophomore year, boys are 12 percent more likely than girls to work 15 or more hours per week. Gradually, however, this gender difference in work patterns nearly disappears. The percentage of students working 15 hours or more per week increases steadily from sophomore to senior year. By senior year, about 60 percent of all students work more than 15 hours a week. Also by senior year, very few differences in these working arrangements are observable across either sex or school type. Generally, there are no significant differences between the two school types with regard to student part-time work. On the basis of the measures considered here, therefore, students in mixed- and single-sex schools do not differ greatly in their behavior outside of school.

Time Spent on Homework

The effects of homework on student achievement are widely debated today. Students, parents, and teachers believe that homework helps students do better in school (Harvard Education Letter, 1985). Unfortunately, research on the issue indicates inconsistent results. Austin (1979) reviewed 80 years of research on math homework and found 16 comparisons favoring homework and 13 showing no differences between students who were assigned homework and those who were not.

The problem with some of the research is that ability grouping accounts for a great deal of the homework that is assigned. In college preparatory tracks, more homework is assigned, and failure to do homework typically leads to low achievement in those tracks. In general and vocational tracks, on the other hand, much less homework is assigned. In these tracks the relationship of homework to achievement may be considerably attenuated. Minimally, it is reasonable to conclude that students who do homework never do worse in school and often do better.

In the HSB sample, important differences exist between the school types with regard to the time students spend on homework. These homework patterns also differ in important ways according to both sex and sample type. The following discussion takes these distinctions into account, although the sample variations are not available in Table 4.3. Sophomores in single-sex schools are 15 percent more likely to do five or more hours of homework a week than sophomores in mixed-sex schools. This is true for both boys and girls in both the regular and minority school samples. In most comparisons, girls average about an hour more of homework a week than boys, except in mixed-sex schools of the minority sample, where boys and girls spend an equal amount of time on homework.

During the senior year this difference between school types drops slightly among students in the regular sample. Females in single-sex schools do 0.8 hour more homework than females in mixed-sex schools, while the difference among males is 0.6 hour, still in favor of single-sex schools. In the minority sample, however, the difference in homework between students in single- and mixed-sex schools remains at a hour more for males, and actually increases to two hours more for females, favoring single-sex schools in both cases. These results for females in both samples are especially salient and merit further attention in the analysis of cognitive outcomes. (These hourly figures are not shown in Table 4.3.)

Homework is generally a school policy variable; that is, it is under the control of the school. Although teachers and the school decide how much homework to assign, the home influences how much of the assigned homework is done. It would be naive to think otherwise. Of course, little homework will be done if little or none is assigned. On the other hand, the fact that a great deal is assigned does not guarantee that a great deal will be done. Thus, both the home and the school influence the amount of homework completed. Fortunately, one can examine the relative effects of the home and the school on homework, using the same multivariate technique used earlier for student attitudes. With that technique I tested the model depicted in Figure 4.2.

Controlling for the influence of the home does not change the results shown in Table 4.3, which allows us to conclude that apparently there are different school policies regarding homework in single- and mixed-sex schools. The effects of home background per se are greater than the effects of school. What is important here, however, is that students in mixed- and single-sex Catholic schools differ in the amount of homework they do, and this difference is not diminished or explained by their differing home background. Moreover, students in single-sex schools in the minority sample do the most homework, by far.

Discipline and Adolescent Values in the Schools

In Chapter 3 we identified two interrelated factors which are likely to favor single-sex schools insofar as academic outcomes are concerned—the adolescent subculture and disciplinary policies of the school. The former refers to the nonschool-centered values of students, such as athletics, social life, and dating. It is widely believed that the

FIGURE 4.2. Modeling the Effects of Home and School on Student Homework

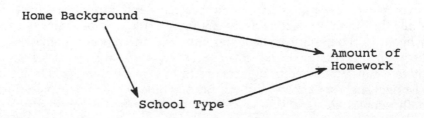

existence and manifestation of this subculture are obstacles to the attainment of educational goals. Likewise, a disciplined and orderly school has been shown to be more effective academically.

Excellent measures of the adolescent subculture and disciplinary context of the schools are available in the HSB survey. One question in particular asked students whether or not they were part of the "leading crowd" at the school. Students were also asked a variety of questions regarding their attitudes toward athletics, social activities, and academics. In addition, as noted earlier, they provided information regarding their dating behaviors. To compute a measure of the adolescent subculture at each school, students who identified themselves as part of the leading crowd were first selected from each school. Then, among these students only, responses to the other questions were aggregated, and that value was assigned to each school. Thus, for each dichotomized item, the percentage of the "leading crowd" in each school leaning in the direction of the adolescent subculture is assigned as an aggregated value to each student in that school. The measure displayed in Table 4.3 is a composite of four items. Mixed-sex schools are assigned an adolescent subculture value without control for sex.

Not surprisingly, the adolescent subculture is fairly prevalent in all of the schools. Over 50 percent of the students in these Catholic schools have positive attitudes toward good athletes, and negative attitudes toward good students, and are heavily involved in dating. Interestingly, all-boys schools manifest the highest degree of the adolescent subculture. Some of this is due to an expected male emphasis on sports. Yet, some of it is unexpected and due to a greater extent of dating among boys in single-sex schools.

By contrast, the adolescent subculture is lower for girls attending single-sex schools than it is for boys. Although these data are not shown in Table 4.3, the adolescent subculture is even less prevalent in girls' single-sex schools in the minority school sample (see Chapter 5). There are some interesting differences across the school types on certain items of the composite measure. Girls in mixed-sex schools are more positively attracted to good athletes and negatively oriented to good students than are girls in single-sex schools. However, girls in single-sex schools are more likely to be dating during the senior year than are girls in mixed-sex schools. On balance, girls in single-sex schools manifest less of the adolescent subculture than girls in mixed-sex schools.

A measure of the disciplinary context of each school was computed in a similar manner. Student responses to the following items were aggregated to the school level: the extent to which students regularly attend school, generally do not cut classes, rarely talk back to teachers, generally obey instructions, rarely fight with each other, and never attack teachers. Thus, each student receives an aggregated value reflecting the percentage of the students in each school who answered affirmatively to the above items. The discipline index shown in Table 4.3 is a composite of the six specific items and represents the average percentage of students in each school type reporting good discipline in the school.

The level of discipline is higher in single- than in mixed-sex schools. Although the difference appears to be small (3–4 percentage points), it is statistically significant (p < .0001). Girls' schools have the highest level of discipline, which can be coupled with the lowest level of adolescent subculture. In girls' schools the adolescent subculture is weak and the discipline is strong, suggesting an environment that is perhaps academically efficient, although a bit overcontrolled. Boys' schools, too, have good discipline. But since the adolescent subculture is high in these schools, the strict discipline is perhaps in response to the subculture.

Although not shown in Table 4.3, the discipline levels in the minority school sample are even more favorable toward single-sex schools. In this sample, the discipline index values are 91 percent in girls' schools, 88 percent in boys' schools, and only 82 percent in mixed-sex schools. Hence, if, as many people believe, strong discipline and order are critical components of effective schooling, students in single-sex schools in the minority sample should perform rather well in comparison with their counterparts in mixed-sex schools. Likewise, the differences in the adolescent value system are greater across the school types in the minority sample.

CONCLUSIONS

The following conclusions may be drawn about the formal and informal characteristics of single- and mixed-sex Catholic schools. Boys in single-sex schools come from homes of higher socioeconomic status and with fewer children than boys in mixed-sex schools. They are also more likely to have mothers who were employed during their school years and to come from an intact two-parent family. They have higher educational expectations and do more homework than boys in mixed-sex schools. Yet, they find time to date and they work more often than students in mixed-sex schools.

Single-sex schools for boys provide stronger discipline than do mixed-sex schools. However, the student value system tends to be less academic in single-sex schools than in mixed-sex schools. The faculty at boys' schools are better trained, more experienced, and better motivated than at mixed-sex schools. The faculty at boys' schools are, of course, mostly male. Finally, single-sex schools for boys have greater financial resources and place more students in a college curriculum than do mixed-sex schools.

Girls in single-sex schools come from homes of slightly lower socioeconomic status and, surprisingly, with fewer children than girls in mixed-sex schools. They are also more likely to have mothers who were employed during their school years. They have higher educational expectations and also do more homework than girls in mixed-sex schools.

Single-sex schools for girls provide very strict discipline, and the student nonacademic value system (adolescent subculture) is weak (especially in the minority sample, as explained in Chapter 5). Compared with those at mixed-sex schools, the faculty at girls' single-sex schools are slightly better trained and slightly more experienced, but are much higher in their commitment and motivation. Most of the faculty in all-girls schools are female. A greater percentage of girls at single-sex schools are placed in a college program than at mixed-sex schools. Single-sex schools for girls operate with relatively modest financial resources that come almost entirely from tuition.

All of this suggests a social psychological environment in single-sex schools that is conducive to high academic performance. We turn now to examine empirically the short-term outcomes of single- and mixed-sex schooling.

Short-Term Outcomes
of Mixed- and
Single-Sex Schooling

This chapter and the following chapter provide reports of several recent empirical investigations of mixed- and single-sex schooling in America. In this chapter, I consider the short-term results of schooling across a variety of outcome measures. In Chapter 6, I take up the long-term outcomes. Data from the high school classes of 1972 and 1982 form the bases for the following empirical analyses. One set of studies examines the differences between Catholic single-sex and Catholic mixed-sex high schools. Another study (described in Chapter 6) compares women's college graduates with women graduates of mixed-sex colleges. Generally, these data indicate that single-sex schools offer educational and occupational advantages for women and minorities. White males, on the other hand, seem to perform slightly better in mixed-sex schools or equally well in either type of school.

One of the great dilemmas in the study of single- and mixed-sex schools is the lack of high-quality data. In fact, the absence of such data makes it quite difficult to resolve the conflicting theoretical positions presented in Chapter 3. Although each of the arguments in Chapter 3 was bolstered or refuted by one study or another, the validity of the data in virtually every study to date is suspect. Several problems are involved in obtaining appropriate data.

The most difficult hurdle, to which I alluded in Chapter 1, is controlling for the likely influence of a student's home background. Students who come from good homes are likely to attend good schools, making it difficult to determine why they turn out to be good students. To estimate the influence of school, therefore, one must have empirical measures of both school type and home background. Along the same lines, it is important to have a measure of each student's initial academic ability that can be compared (or controlled) when assessing academic results at the completion of schooling. And, of course, it is vital that the data of a study be truly representative of a set of schools, that is, that the study be based on a random sample. Unfortunately, most of the research reviewed in Chapter 3 does not meet all three of these conditions. Fortunately, however, data exist to meet this challenge.

DESIGN OF THE STUDY

The Data

In 1972, the National Center for Education Statistics (NCES) began an ambitious program of research with a project called the National Longitudinal Study of the High School Class of 1972 (NLS). This study involved 22,652 graduating senior students in 1318 private, public, and church-related schools. These students were randomly selected through a two-stage stratified sampling strategy. First, schools were randomly selected, and then students from each school were randomly identified. In 1972, these students completed a base-year questionnaire and an extensive test battery. In addition to the student questionnaires, a variety of valuable data were gathered from the high school records. Follow-up studies on these students were conducted in 1973, 1974, 1976, 1979, and 1986. In Chapter 6 this data set is used to study long-term effects.

In 1980, NCES initiated a second long-term study of high school students, which came to be called High School and Beyond (HSB). This is a longitudinal study of 58,270 high school sophomores and seniors who were randomly selected through the same type of two-stage stratified sampling strategy as described above for the NLS data. In this chapter, I use only the HSB sophomores, who as seniors became the high school graduating class of 1982. These students ($N=29,737$) were selected from 1015 public, private, and church-related secondary schools. As with the NLS study, the HSB data contain a broad set of student- and school-reported information.

Thus, the data sets are the high school graduating classes of 1972 (NLS) and 1982 (HSB). One of the major advantages of the NLS study is that follow-ups are available through 1986, which allow us to investigate, in Chapter 6, the longer-term effects of schooling. The major advantage of the HSB study is that test scores are available for the students in both the sophomore and senior years, and this allows for tighter and more valid control in measuring the overall effects of either the school or the home on cognitive outcomes. This is the highest-quality survey data available, and both studies have been the main data source for many educational books and articles.

What kinds of questions were the respondents asked? They are mainly of three kinds, which we can call "background," "schoolground," and "foreground" questions. Among the questions asked about respondents' backgrounds are their race, sex, the socioeconomic characteristics of their parents, and features of the place where they were raised. The "schoolground" questions deal with the students' past and current attachments and accomplishments in school—their course work, curriculum, grades, and extracurricular activities. Then the respondents were asked about their current situation—their foreground, including recent work and family activities, academic progress and plans, and the attitudes they hold toward themselves and others. Among the most interesting research done with the NLS and HSB data is that relating background to foreground, for example, "what kind" of respondents are more likely to graduate from college or to score low on the SAT; or that relating schoolground to foreground, for example, the effect of teachers' expectations or type of school on current academic ability or final educational or occupational attainment.

The Samples

Two types of Catholic schools were sampled in the HSB study. First, a regular Catholic school sample was drawn using a two-stage stratified probability technique. This sample was stratified according to the four census regions of the country, with the schools serving as the first-stage unit and students within the schools as the second-stage unit. In this second stage, 36 students were randomly selected from each school. This regular sample (allowing for nonresponse and missing information) contains 45 schools and 1458 students. In addition to the regular Catholic school sample, HSB drew a stratum of Catholic schools with a high proportion of black or Hispanic students. This sample includes 39 schools and 1251 students.

The actual racial make-up of the regular and the minority Catholic school samples is shown in Table 5.1. Schools in the regular sample are predominantly white; minorities constitute less than 10 percent of the student body. In contrast, white students in the special minority sample constitute only 22 to 44 percent of the populations of these schools. Overall, the minority schools are about one-third white, one-third black, and one-third Hispanic. The only notable exception to this pattern is found among female single-sex schools, which are 46 percent Hispanic and only 22 percent white. Thus, the racial/ethnic context of the two

TABLE 5.1. Racial and Socioeconomic Composition of Students in Catholic Mixed- and Single-Sex Schools[a]

	Regular Sample				Minority Sample			
	Males		Females		Males		Females	
	Mixed	Single	Mixed	Single	Mixed	Single	Mixed	Single
Percent White	91	87	90	86	36	44	34	22
Percent Black	2	3	3	4	25	31	29	29
Percent Hispanic	6	9	6	8	35	24	37	46
Average Socioeconomic Status[b]	.33	.46	.29	.25	.19	.20	.12	-.06
Percent Family 1982 Income Above $25,000	67	79	65	65	51	56	52	44
Number of Students	349	287	382	421	134	398	169	503
Number of Schools	23	9	23	13	10	13	10	16

a Percentages are based on a weighted sample and represent population estimates. Numbers of students and schools are unweighted.

b A composite of five equally weighted standardized components: family yearly income, father's education, mother's education, father's occupation (using Duncan's occupational status scale), and eight household items. The overall public and Catholic school mean is zero.

85

samples is dramatically different. Students in the regular sample attend mostly all-white schools, while students in the special sample attend racially integrated schools.

In addition to these differences in racial context of the samples, the socioeconomic contexts are, not surprisingly, also quite disparate (see Table 5.1). Table 5.1 indicates that the socioeconomic background of students in the regular sample is always higher than that of students in the special minority sample, regardless of sex or school type. This finding is not at all surprising given the nature of the two samples; it provides further support for the decision to analyze the two samples separately. The regular school sample includes a larger percentage of students from high socioeconomic status families. Across both school types, 43 percent of the students in the regular sample come from the higher (top one-fourth) socioeconomic status, as opposed to 30 percent of the students in the minority school sample. In the regular sample, 68 percent of the students come from homes with a total family income above $25,000, compared with 50 percent of the students in the minority sample. Thus, the two samples differ not only in racial context but also in socioeconomic climate.

Moreover, the number of single-sex schools in the minority sample is disproportionate to the number in the total Catholic school population. In the minority school sample, 74 percent of the schools are single-sex institutions. By comparison, 49 percent of the schools in the regular school sample are single-sex, which is fairly close to the actual population parameter for Catholic single-sex secondary schools (42 percent) (Coleman, Hoffer, & Kilgore, 1982, p. 26, Table 2–7). Finally, there are additional background differences across the samples, as noted in Chapter 4.

Consequently, I chose to analyze these samples separately. Other researchers have combined the two samples (Alexander & Pallas, 1985; Bryk, Holland, Lee, & Carriedo, 1984; Coleman et al., 1982; Greeley, 1982; Hoffer, Greeley, & Coleman, 1985; Lee & Bryk, 1986) and controlled for race in the analysis. Several of these investigators (Lee & Bryk, 1986; Willms, 1985) have controlled statistically for the different racial/ethnic and socioeconomic context of these schools. I proceed by comparing outcomes between students in single-sex and mixed-sex schools in each of the samples separately (technically, the samples are partitioned). In the regular school sample, I consider white students only, because there are simply too few minority students. In the minority sample, I concentrate on the results for black and Hispanic students. Regardless of whether one partitions the samples or controls for them statistically, the results for females are similar. For males, however, the effects of school type differ according to school sample, and this fact is masked when only a statistical control is employed. This latter finding has important theoretical implications.

The study uses data for students who completed the test batteries in both years. Dropouts are excluded. Transfer students and early graduates, however, are included. Less than 3 percent of the Catholic school sample transferred to other schools. I have assumed that many of these people transferred to a similar school type and that the small number of students who transferred to a different school type will not bias the results.

The Strategy of the Analysis

The first step in the analysis was to determine the gender context policy of the sampled schools, that is, whether they were single- or mixed-sex schools. This was accomplished by aggregating the ratio of male to female students in each school. Each school was examined to determine whether it was composed of students of the same sex or of both sexes. Given that the sample attempted to draw 36 students from each school, it is very unlikely that a school would be 100 percent of a single sex in the sample, unless that was the school policy. Hence, any school that met this criterion was treated as a single-sex school in this study. As a further check, however, the school type identified in this manner was confirmed by the use of a school-level question that specifically asked (of the school administration) for the percentage of female students in the school.

The basic strategy in the analysis of short-term outcomes is to determine first the raw uncontrolled effect of school type on each of the outcome variables. In the HSB survey, an extensive variety of cognitive and affective measures are used for this purpose. This uncontrolled effect, however large it may appear, may result from the fact that single-sex schools may attract and select better students. Hence, the next step is to adjust the raw differences across school type in order to account for initial differences in ability and differences in home background.

At this point, remaining differences across school types can reasonably be attributed to the school. Those differences can be adjusted finally for a variety of school variables that may help to explain the school type effect. Presuming we find that students in single-sex schools outperform students in mixed-sex schools, we want to know why. Is it due to differences in curriculum placement, course work, or homework?

Or possibly to a reduced adolescent subculture and/or a stricter disciplinary environment? The strategy is depicted schematically in Figure 5.1.

It is, of course, hoped that by comparing outcomes for students
with parental socioeconomic status estimated to be the same (parents'
education, income, and so on), the students in different schools will be
"equated" in terms of their background, and that any differences found
in outcomes can then be attributed to something different about the
school. This effort is certainly not foolproof, for it is seldom possible to
control on all relevant background characteristics. The possibility always
remains that the differences attributed to school type might be due
instead to some unmeasured aspect of the students' background.

This is a problem that all studies of school effects must inevitably
face. It is the problem of separating the effects of the home and initial
student competencies from the effect of the school. Good schools may
be more attractive initially to good students. Alexander and Pallas (1983)
summarize this possibility succinctly.

> Probably the single greatest burden of school effects research is to dis-
> tinguish convincingly between outcome differences that reflect simple
> differences in the kinds of students who attend various schools from
> differences that are attributable to something about the schools them-
> selves. . . . Put simply, when good students go to good schools, how are
> we to know which is responsible for the good performance that is likely
> to be observed? (p. 170)

The answer is that one must control or adjust for student differences
that may be relevant to the outcomes being investigated. These differences include initial academic competency or achievement, socioeconomic background, and race/ethnicity. Typically, high performance is
associated with both higher socioeconomic background and a hypothesized more effective school. Boys (but not girls) in single-sex schools

FIGURE 5.1. Modeling the Educational Process

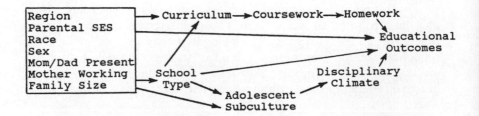

come from homes of above-average socioeconomic status, and their initial abilities are higher than those of boys in mixed-sex schools on all the cognitive tests. It is necessary, therefore, to adjust the test score outcomes by controlling for home background and initial ability. We must know what the test score gains would be if each school type enrolled students from the same home backgrounds and with the same initial abilities.

An *estimate* of this everybody-is-the-same scenario can be computed using statistical controls in a regression equation. Essentially, a regression equation determines the effect of certain predictor or independent variables on a dependent variable while controlling for all other predictor variables. The reader may find the example in the Appendix helpful.

Tests of Significance

Usually in research of this type, a statistical "test of significance" can be used to determine the likelihood that a school effect found in the sample is large enough so that we can generally infer that the effect is significantly greater than zero in the entire population. Assume, for example, that students in single-sex schools score 0.6 of a grade equivalent higher than students in mixed-sex schools in the sample. Since every sample contains some degree of sampling error, it is possible that the true effect in the population is actually higher or lower than 0.6 of a grade equivalent. For any sample, it is possible to estimate the likely amount of error, which is referred to as the standard error. Assume that in the above example the standard error is 0.2 of a grade equivalent. Generally, social scientists prefer that a sample statistic (in this case, the school effect) be at least two times the standard error. Statistically speaking, the probability is that 95 times out of 100, the actual population effect will be plus or minus two standard errors of the sample effect. In the above example, we could say with 95 percent confidence that the interval between 0.2 and 1.0 contained the true population value. This is sort of a backwards way of saying that the effect is significantly greater than zero.

Given the research strategy that I have chosen to employ, however, problems arise regarding the use of significance tests. Having divided the regular and minority sample, and choosing to analyze boys and girls separately, we decrease all the sample sizes considerably. Table 5.1 displays the maximum number of students in each sample and school type who could actually be considered in the analysis. When these subsamples are disaggregated by race and other background characteristics, the situation becomes more troublesome. These numbers are reduced further by missing data, which invariably exist on certain of the variables. The upshot of this is that the estimate of standard errors is constrained. Standard errors are a function of both effect size and sample size. Even small effects may be significant if the sample size is large; on the other hand, large effects may not be significant if the sample size is small. In these data, the standard errors are large, making the sample effects appear insignificant.

This problem could be eliminated, at least partly, by pooling the regular and minority samples. This would double the sample size; in fact, under this strategy, most of the sample effects, which are reasonably large, are significant. Lee and Bryk (1986) chose this strategy, and their results confirm this. The statistical significance of school effects for the pooled data is pivotal, especially because the size of the effects is consistent with those obtained using separate samples. The significance is due to the larger sample size, which decreases the standard error. The problem, however, is that pooling the samples conceals the contextual differences between them. Moreover, it masks some important differential results, which I will report. Both the samples and the results are different, and the best course of action is to analyze them separately.

This means a sacrifice of the luxury that comes from being able to claim overall statistical significance of one's findings. Even with this caveat, however, half of the short-term effects and most of the long-term effects for females are significant. Readers who are uneasy about the generality of the findings should refer to the work of Lee and Bryk (1986), who, because they pooled the two samples, were better able to demonstrate the statistical significance of the results. Caution is advised, however, regarding the pooled results for males in the Lee and Bryk (1986) study.

A question also remains regarding the size of an effect, regardless of its statistical significance. Is a 0.3 of a grade equivalent difference between school types noteworthy? Over this issue, there is even greater controversy (see Alexander & Pallas, 1983, 1984, 1985; Hoffer, Greeley, & Coleman, 1985; Kilgore, 1983, 1984). There is simply no way of satisfying everyone on this issue. My view is that any effect that looks like it might amount to about 0.5 of a grade equivalent over a four-year high school period is important. It is the difference between graduating and not graduating, attending and not attending college, a high school graduate and a high school dropout, a more effective and a less effective school.

COGNITIVE OUTCOMES

We turn our attention first to the primary objective of schooling—
cognitive development. In the study of school effects, the dependent
variable of central interest is how much students have learned. This
question concerns educators, parents, policy makers, and students.

The Cognitive Tests

The Educational Testing Service (ETS) designed the cognitive test
battery for the HSB survey. It includes seven tests: three achievement
tests designed to measure basic skills in vocabulary, reading, and mathematics, and four curriculum-dependent tests in mathematics, writing,
science, and civics. The tests of basic skills were not intended to cover
explicit parts of the school curriculum in the last two years of high
school (Coleman et al., 1982; Heynes & Hilton, 1982). Rather, these
general tests were meant to "serve as predictors and covariates in studies
of career development, academic attainment and job performance"
(Heynes & Hilton, 1982, p. 90). In the initial version of the test battery,
all the tests were elementary and not dependent on exposure to particular high school courses. Subsequent revisions, however, made four of the
tests specifically curriculum-dependent so that studies of school effects
could be conducted.

Thus, four tests specifically measure skills taught during the last
two years of high school. The scores on these four curriculum-specific
tests are the main measures of cognitive outcomes used in this book.
The specific tests include

> *Advanced Mathematics,* a 10-item test of skills in algebra, geometry,
> and trigonometry
> *Writing,* a 17-item test of writing ability and knowledge of basic
> grammar
> *Science,* a 20-item test of science knowledge and science reasoning
> ability
> *Civics,* a 10-item test on various principles of law, government, and
> social behavior

Although some researchers (Alexander & Pallas, 1985; Coleman et
al., 1982; Hoffer et al., 1985) have treated the general tests as dependent
outcome measures, others (Heynes & Hilton, 1982; Willms, 1985) argue
that the curriculum-specific tests are the most appropriate measures for

assessing school effects. Thus, the four curriculum-specific tests are the main focus of this section. Basically, the results are the same regardless of the number of tests considered (see also Lee & Bryk, 1986).

The test results reported here are for students in the college and general tracks only. Students in these tracks constitute nearly 95 percent of all students in the schools. I begin with the results for whites only in the regular Catholic school sample, followed by a similar analysis for Hispanics and blacks in the specially selected minority Catholic school sample. For all tests, I use what are referred to as formula scores. These are raw scores, reflecting the number of correct answers, adjusted for guessing.

The Regular Catholic School Sample

The analysis begins by considering white students only in the regular sample. This sample contains 13 girls' schools, 9 boys' schools, and 23 mixed-sex schools. The number of students in the regression analysis varies with the test, sex, and school type. The ranges of the sample size are 350–472 for males and 477–619 for females. These numbers are less than those shown in Table 5.1 due to a loss of cases with missing information on some of the variables.

Table 5.2 displays the adjusted senior-year test score differences between white students in the regular Catholic single- and mixed-sex schools. A positive score indicates that students in single-sex schools outperform students in mixed-sex schools, while a negative score means the reverse. From left to right, Table 5.2 first presents the unadjusted difference, separately for males and females. This unadjusted difference represents the effect of school type on the senior-year test scores, before adjustment for home background and initial ability. Next come the results adjusted first for initial ability and then for both ability and home background. The home background adjustment includes the socioeconomic composite plus region, family structure, family size, and the work patterns of mothers.

All the data in Table 5.2 are expressed as grade equivalents, thus permitting comparisons among the tests and/or between males and females. The average raw score increment that students attain on each test over a school year is generally known as the grade equivalent of a test. In this case, the increment is the average end-of-sophomore- to end-of-senior-year gain for all students combined, divided by two (the average increase made on each test during a single year). For each specific test, the single-sex minus the mixed-sex school difference is divided by the average one-year grade equivalent. Assuming that this gain is con-

TABLE 5.2. Adjusted Senior-Year Test Score Differences Between White Students in Regular Mixed- and Single-Sex Catholic Schools (Expressed as a Percentage of One Grade Year Equivalent)

Curriculum-Specific Tests	Males (N = 350-472)			Females (N = 477-619)		
	Unadjusted Senior-Year Difference[a]	Adjusted for Initial Ability[b]	Adjusted for Initial Ability and Home Background[c]	Unadjusted Senior-Year Difference[a]	Adjusted for Initial Ability[b]	Adjusted for Initial Ability and Home Background[c]
Advanced Math	1.3	0.4	0.3	0.5	0.3	0.2
Writing	0.8	-0.2	-0.8	0.3	0.4	0.2*
Science	1.0	0.7	0.3	0.5	0.9	0.9*
Civics	0.3	0.0	-0.3	0.6	0.6	0.6*

[a] Computed from a bivariate regression of test score on school type.

[b] This adjustment included only the specific pre-test as a control.

[c] This adjustment involved the following controls: the specific pre-test plus region, socioeconomic status, family structure, family size, and family work structure.

* Sig. $p < 0.05$

stant over a four-year high school program, one would double each gain to obtain an estimate of the overall high school effect.

In Table 5.2, we see that by the end of the senior year both males and females in single-sex schools score higher than their same-sex peers in mixed-sex schools across all tests. With only one exception, the advantage for males in single-sex schools is considerably greater than the advantage held by females in single-sex schools. Generally, these raw differences are more than a grade equivalent for males and one-half of a grade equivalent for females. These unadjusted differences change dramatically, however, when controls are added for initial ability and home background.

Adjusting for Initial Ability and Home Background.   In the case of males, after the control variables have been added, the original advantage of the single-sex school disappears. Specifically, while the average unadjusted difference across the four curriculum tests was 0.9 in favor of single-sex schools, the adjusted (for both ability and background) average across these four tests is 0.1 in favor of mixed-sex schools. In general, half of the unadjusted difference can be accounted for by initial ability and the other half by home background. Thus, Table 5.2 shows no appreciable school type effect on short-term cognitive outcomes for boys.

Females, however, appear to be positively affected in single-sex schools. As noted above, girls in single-sex schools show an unadjusted advantage of one-half of a grade equivalent across all tests. Girls in single- and mixed-sex schools differ little in initial academic ability and home background. Hence, we would not expect the test score differences to change drastically when adjusted for these controlling factors. This is, in fact, the case. After adjusting for initial ability and home background, as shown in Table 5.2, girls in single-sex schools continue to score 0.5 grade equivalent higher than girls in mixed-sex schools on the four curriculum-specific tests. Most remarkable is the test score difference in science of almost one (0.9) grade equivalent or perhaps two full years over the four-year high school stretch.

The Effects of the Formal School Structure.   In the regular Catholic school sample, girls do better in single-sex schools, and boys do equally well in either school type. Presumably, school policies and school climate account for some of these differences. The most obvious factors are curriculum, course work, and homework. In all likelihood the students who do well are more apt to be in a college track, to have been exposed to more rigorous course work, and to have consistently spent more time on their homework. In addition to these aspects of the formal school structure, which we will consider first, there may be informal differences across school type in terms of the presence or absence of an adolescent subculture. Table 5.3 continues the process of adjustment by adding to the regression equation the variables of track, course work, homework, and the adolescent context.

Students in college preparatory programs are more likely to pursue advanced course work in all subject areas. Consequently, there are differences in the courses students take in mixed- and single-sex schools. In general, these course-work differences are surprisingly small except in mathematics, where students in single-sex schools get far more exposure to advanced courses than students in mixed-sex schools. For each test, the extent of course work in the specific subject was determined and

TABLE 5.3. Adjusted Senior-Year Test Score Differences Between White Students in Regular Mixed- and Single-Sex Catholic Schools (Expressed as a Percentage of One Grade Year Equivalent)

Curriculum-Specific Tests	Adjusted for Initial Ability and Home Background	(+)	Adjusted for Track[a] and Course work[b]	(+)	Adjusted for Homework[c]	(+)	Adjusted for Adolescent Context[d]
MALES							
Advanced Math	0.3		0.1		0.1		0.0
Writing	−0.8		−0.9		−0.8		−0.9
Science	0.3		0.2		0.2		0.0
Civics	−0.3		−0.4		−0.3		−0.5
FEMALES							
Advanced Math	0.2		0.1		−0.2		−0.2
Writing	0.2*		0.2		0.2		0.1
Science	0.9*		0.8		1.0		0.9
Civics	0.6*		0.5		0.4		0.3

[a] Student-reported track placement as of the sophomore survey.

[b] This adjustment includes course work in the specific test area; i.e., course work in math for the math test, course work in science for the science test, and so forth.

[c] Includes amount of homework per week reported in both the sophomore and senior years averaged as a single score.

[d] A variable aggregated to the school level based on "leading crowd" student responses regarding the extent of dating in the sophomore year, going steady or engaged in the sophomore year, attitudes toward students with good grades, and attitudes toward athletic students. A high score on this variable reflects a greater manifestation of the adolescent subculture.

* Sig. $p < 0.05$

applied as a further control. On the writing test, for example, the number of half-years of English from the tenth to the twelfth grade was used.

It turns out, however, that course work exposure has very little effect on test score outcomes, despite the differences in course work across the two school types. Presumably, the potential influence of course work is removed by first controlling for track. Students in the same track generally take the same courses. For this reason, I have included the effects of track and course work together in Table 5.3. Another possibility is that the content of the courses may differ across tracks (Oakes, 1985). A simple measure of the number of courses taken by a student may underestimate the true difference among courses of the same name in different tracks.

For girls, the inclusion of track reduces the single-sex school advantage. As noted earlier, girls in single-sex schools are somewhat more likely than girls in mixed-sex schools to pursue a college track, and their curriculum placement explains a portion of the single-sex school advantage. For boys, the overall effect of track across the four tests is to increase the average mixed-sex school advantage. On two tests, the single-sex school advantage is reduced by 0.1 of a grade equivalent; on the other two, the mixed-sex school advantage is increased by the same amount. The average increase in the mixed-sex school advantage derives from the fact that boys in mixed-sex schools actually do better in writing and civics, even though fewer of them are in a college track. The regression adjustment informs us, not surprisingly, that they would do even better if they enrolled in a college track at the equivalent rate of boys in single-sex schools. In fact (as noted in Chapter 4), students in single-sex schools are about 10 percent more likely to be in a college track than students in mixed-sex schools. Thus, the inclusion of track reduces the average grade equivalent advantage (across the tests) for females in single-sex schools from 0.5 to 0.4, while the average test score advantage for boys in mixed-sex schools increases from 0.1 to 0.2.

In Chapter 4 we noted that students in single-sex schools (especially girls) did more homework than students in mixed-sex schools during the sophomore year. By the senior year, this difference decreases slightly for both boys and girls in the regular Catholic school sample. Surprisingly, Table 5.3 shows that the amount of homework done has only a modest effect on previously existing differences. Three test score differences decrease by 0.1, one increases by 0.2, three remain the same. Among girls the effect of homework makes a difference as great as 0.3 of a grade equivalent on the math test. Averaged across all four tests, the addition of homework explains very little of the test score differences between the school types.

On the science test the 0.2 increase favoring single-sex schools for girls is due to the fact that homework actually has a small negative effect on the senior science test score, thus favoring those students who do less homework. This finding is consistent with a pattern pointing to the greater importance of the environment of the single-sex school over that of the home. Although girls in single-sex schools do more homework than girls in mixed-sex schools, the science test score advantage is apparently a function of what is learned in school rather than at home. It is also conceivable that students do less science homework than in other subjects. Thus, the amount of homework they report is largely unrelated to what they actually learn about science.

Within the limits of the HSB data, we have now exhausted the *formal* means whereby schools may influence academic outcomes. School policies of track placement, course work, and homework explain some of the existing differences across school types. The only exception is the math test, where school policies explain virtually all of the single-sex advantage for both boys and girls. For the other three tests, school policy variables explain only a small amount of the existing school effect. Averaged across all four tests, the three formal school variables explain about 0.1 of the background-adjusted differences between the school types.

The Effects of the Social Environment of the School. The adolescent subculture (discussed in Chapters 3 and 4) concerns *informal*, student-generated norms dictating behavior antithetical to the formal norms of the school. The adolescent subculture centers on athletics, social life, and dating. The HSB study involved strenuous efforts to obtain data on the adolescent subculture.

The following questions generated a measure of the adolescent subculture, aggregated to the school level:

1. Are you seen by other sophomores as part of the leading crowd?
2. How often do you spend time going out on dates?
3. Are you going steady with one person or engaged?
4. How do you feel toward good students?
5. How do you feel toward athletic students?

Students were first selected who were, in fact, part of the leading crowd. Responses to the leading crowd question were "very," "somewhat," and "not at all." If possible, the aggregated variable was constructed among students indicating that they were "very" much part of the leading crowd. This was possible for 73 percent of the schools. For the remaining schools, it was necessary to include students who were only "somewhat" part of the leading crowd. On average, about 60 percent of the students defined themselves as part of the leading crowd.

Then, from among these leading crowd students only, responses to the remaining four questions were aggregated to the school level; for example, if 60 percent of students in the leading crowd answered yes to question 3 at a specific school, then the school was coded as 60 percent. This means, in effect, that all students at this school are assigned this value. (Questions 2, 4, and 5 were dichotomized.) The assumptions are that the leading crowd is the center of the subculture and that its value (high or low) may influence anyone, even those outside the clique. The value of the variable was coded high for a subcultural response. Thus, dating, negative feelings toward good students, and positive feelings toward athletes are scored high. For each respondent, the values on each of the four items (2, 3, 4, 5) were combined to form a single adolescent subculture variable.

The adolescent subculture is most widespread among boys in single-sex schools and is least manifest in single-sex schools for girls. Boys and girls in mixed-sex schools have the same value of the subculture, although it varies slightly when boys and girls are considered separately. Mixed-sex schools are assigned an adolescent subculture value without control for sex. The average value for boys and girls in mixed-sex schools differs slightly, however, due to variation in the male–female ratio of the schools. Specifically, there are a few more girls in mixed-sex schools with a higher adolescent subculture value. This makes the difference across the school types slightly greater for each sex than is shown below. The percentages of leading crowd students in the respective school types providing an adolescent subcultural response to the combination of questions 2, 3, 4, and 5 were as follows:

Male single-sex schools	58.96
Mixed-sex schools	53.92
Female single-sex schools	53.22

The effects of the adolescent subculture relate positively to all test scores for boys, and negatively for girls. For boys, higher test scores are associated with *higher* adolescent values; for girls, higher test scores are associated with *lower* adolescent subculture values. However, school type relates positively to the adolescent subculture for boys, and negatively for girls. Among boys, an adolescent subculture is more prevalent in single-sex than in mixed-sex schools; among girls, an adolescent subculture is slightly more prevalent in mixed-sex schools. Hence, the effects of adjusting for the adolescent subculture are generally to increase the indirect positive effects of school type, and conversely to decrease the direct effect. Figure 5.2 illustrates this process.

The results show a reduction in the final single-sex school advantage for boys in math and science to zero, while the already existing mixed-sex school advantage in writing and civics increases (see Table 5.3). The same general effect is shown among girls, for whom three of the four tests show a small reduction in the single-sex advantage. Overall, the effects of an adolescent subculture average about 0.1 of a grade equivalent for boys and girls together; that is, a less intense adolescent subculture explains about as much of the background-adjusted differences across school types as the formal school characteristics do. It should be noted that these formal and informal explanations of the school type effect are substantial, even though they may appear to be small. This issue will be discussed further in the chapter.

The effect of a high adolescent subculture is negative for girls, yet it is positive for boys. Since two of the four items in the subculture scale concern dating patterns, an increase in cross-sex relations outside of school, especially serious relationships, may have a positive effect on the academic performance of boys. It appears that an increased adolescent context for boys correlates with a more ordered and disciplined school environment. The disciplinary environment of the schools was measured by questions on the extent of not attending school, cutting classes, talking back to teachers, disobeying instructions, and fighting among students. This variable, like the adolescent subculture, was aggregated to the school level, with a high score on the variable indicating greater discipline and order. The correlation between the adolescent subculture and school discipline for boys was +0.09, whereas for girls the correlation was −0.39 in the regular Catholic school sample. Single-sex schools for girls involve a low adolescent subculture and a high degree of disci-

FIGURE 5.2. Modeling the Effect of the Adolescent Subculture by Sex

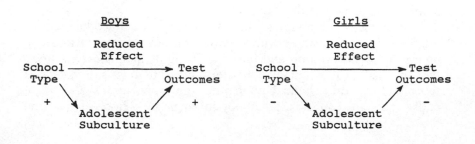

pline. Single-sex schools for boys, on the other hand, have a high adolescent subculture and a fairly high degree of discipline.

We can only speculate as to why this is so. The relationship for boys is straightforward — in order to effectively control an academic environment containing a strong adolescent subculture, it is reasonable to expect schools to implement strong disciplinary policies. But why do we find very strong disciplinary codes in single-sex schools that manifest low values of the adolescent subculture? Quite possibly and simply, the schools may be overcontrolled, providing an unnecessarily high level of discipline. This certainly fits the stereotyped image of girls' Catholic high schools. In Chapter 3, we noted that Schneider and Coutts (1982) also found that single-sex schools for girls emphasize a high degree of discipline and control.

As a final step in the analysis, the disciplinary context of the school was added as a control variable. Although the discipline variable has a small positive *zero order* association with test score outcomes, the relationship proved spurious when added to the regression equation for both boys and girls. The relationship of disciplinary environment to senior-year test scores has a number of common causes; namely, home background, initial ability, and school type. The common cause impact is great enough that in several instances the relationship of discipline to test score results is significantly negative, causing the direct effect of school type to actually increase. In six of eight comparisons, however, the effect of disciplinary context is zero, causing no change in the influence of school type on test scores. These results are not included in Table 5.3.

Thus, in the final analysis, the results in Table 5.3 show that after adjusting for initial ability, home background, school policies, and school environment, girls in single-sex schools outperform girls in mixed-sex schools by an average of 0.3 of a grade equivalent. For boys, the opposite holds true. Boys in mixed-sex schools outperform boys in single-sex schools by 0.4 of a grade equivalent, on average. These effects would have to be explained by factors other than those we have already considered. These results are for white students only, in the predominantly white regular Catholic school sample.

Of course, we should not overlook the results obtained before adding the school policy and environmental variables. After adjusting simply for home background and initial ability, girls in single-sex schools score one-half (0.5) of a grade equivalent higher than girls in mixed-sex schools. On the other hand, boys in mixed-sex schools test slightly higher (0.1 of a grade equivalent) than boys in single-sex schools. This represents the effect of school type, regardless of our ability to explain how or why it comes about.

The Special Minority Sample

The sample for the specially selected and predominantly minority Catholic schools comprises 16 girls' schools, 13 boys' schools, and 10 mixed-sex schools. On average, the student composition of these schools is about equally divided among blacks, whites, and Hispanics. As with the regular school sample, the analysis includes only students in the college and general tracks. The ranges of the sample size are 200–283 for males and 254–366 for females.

In order to easily focus on minority student outcomes in these predominantly minority schools, whites were excluded entirely from the following analyses. Table 5.4 displays the adjusted senior-year test score differences between minority (black and Hispanic) students in single- and mixed-sex schools in the minority school sample. All the data in Table 5.4 are expressed as grade equivalents, thus permitting comparisons across sex and the two samples.

Adjusting for Initial Ability and Home Background. Table 5.4 shows that students in single-sex schools (both males and females) score higher than their same-sex peers in mixed-sex schools after controlling for initial ability and home background. The only exception is that girls in mixed-sex schools outperform girls in single-sex schools in the advanced math test. The *unadjusted* difference is zero for boys and 1.4 of a grade equivalent for girls, on average, over four tests. After controlling for initial ability, race, and the home background variables, however, the average test score advantage for boys in single-sex schools increases to 0.7. For girls in single-sex schools the average test score advantage decreases to 0.8 after the controls have been added.

These differences are greater than any of the effects found among students in the regular school sample (see Table 5.2). The average size of these effects is three-fourths (.75) of a grade equivalent over a two-year period; or a one and one-half (1.5) grade year difference in favor of single-sex schools over a four-year period, assuming that the pattern held.

Table 5.4 shows differential results for boys and girls when a control for initial ability is added. For boys, the adjustment for initial test score ability has no effect on the unadjusted difference. This reflects the fact that, for black and Hispanic boys, initial sophomore test scores are virtually identical in both school types. On the other hand, minority

TABLE 5.4. Adjusted Senior-Year Test Score Differences Between Minority Students in Predominantly Minority Mixed- and Single-Sex Catholic Schools (Expressed as a Percentage of One Grade Year Equivalent)

Curriculum-Specific Tests	Males (N = 200-283)			Females (N = 254-366)		
	Unadjusted Senior-Year Difference[a]	Adjusted for Initial Ability[b]	Adjusted for Initial Ability, Race, and Home Background[c]	Unadjusted Senior-Year Difference[a]	Adjusted for Initial Ability[b]	Adjusted for Initial Ability, Race, and home Background[c]
Advanced Math	0.6	0.4	1.5*	0.1	-0.5	-0.6
Writing	0.5	0.5	0.8	1.1	0.2	0.3*
Science	-0.7	-0.7	0.3	2.2	1.5	1.5*
Civics	-0.3	-0.3	0.2	2.3	1.8	1.9*

a Computed from a bivariate regression of test score on school type.

b This adjustment included only the specific pre-test as a control.

c This adjustment involved the following controls: the specific pre-test plus region, socioeconomic status, family structure, race (black, Hispanic), family size, and family work structure.

* Sig. p < 0.05

boys in single-sex schools are disadvantaged in terms of home background. Considering the entire sample (Hispanics, blacks, and whites), boys in mixed- and single-sex schools come from fairly similar socioeconomic status homes (see Table 5.1). Among Hispanics and blacks, however, students in single-sex schools come from homes of lower socioeconomic status. Therefore, when adjustments are added for the home background variables, the adjusted single-sex test score advantage is increased. For boys, the adjusted result is 0.7 of a grade equivalent single-sex school advantage.

For girls, the effects of the adjustment process are different. The initial test scores of Hispanic females are fairly close in both school types, while black females initially scored higher in single-sex schools. Therefore, the average test score difference favoring females in single-sex schools decreases to 0.8, after adjusting for initial ability. Part of the single-sex school advantage is explained by differences in initial ability. On the other hand, including home background as a control variable slightly increases the adjusted test score advantage of girls in single-sex schools. Hispanic girls in single-sex schools come from homes of very low socioeconomic status; the socioeconomic background of black females is slightly higher in single-sex schools. On balance, black and Hispanic females in single-sex schools are slightly disadvantaged in the home background variables. Consequently, the adjusted average test score advantage for females in single-sex schools increases slightly when home background is considered, but still remains 0.8 of a grade equivalent advantage when rounded off.

To repeat, these adjusted differences are quite substantial. Unlike the results in the regular school sample among whites only, in the minority school sample *both* boys and girls in single-sex schools outperform students in mixed-sex schools. These results hold after controlling for initial ability and home background. Thus it appears as if the effects of school type are greater among minorities, and this has often been shown to be true. It was established, perhaps initially, by Coleman et al. (1966) in their famous study, *Equality of Educational Opportunity*. In that national study in the United States, the overall effects of school quality were found to be small. Among whites, differences among schools explained only 7.4 percent of the variance in cognitive tests. Among minorities (black, Hispanic, Native Americans), however, school effects doubled and tripled those of whites (see Coleman et al., 1966, p. 299, Tables 3.221.1 and 3.221.2).

Likewise, in her study of summer learning, Heynes (1978) observed that the effects of school are greatest among poor children. She found that children of above-average means enjoyed cognitive gains whether schools were in session (academic year) or not (summer). More recently, studies using the HSB data show that the magnitude of Catholic school effects, compared with public schools, is larger for black, Hispanic, and low socioeconomic status students (Greeley, 1982; Hoffer et al., 1985). Thus, the fact that the gender context effect is greater among minorities is not surprising.

The Effects of the Formal and Informal School Structure. As in the case of the regular school sample, I continue the process of adjustment (via regression) by adding variables that measure both the formal and informal structure of school. The formal school structure is represented by measures of curriculum, course work, and homework. The informal school atmosphere is indicated by a measure of the adolescent subculture. Essentially, the purpose of adding these variables is to identify, if possible, the specific mechanisms whereby students in single-sex schools generally score higher on cognitive tests than students in mixed-sex schools. The results appear in Table 5.5.

In the minority sample, students in single-sex schools are about 12 percent more likely to pursue a college preparatory track than students in mixed-sex schools. Likewise, boys in single-sex schools take more course work in math, science, and social studies than boys in mixed-sex schools. Girls in single-sex schools take more course work only in social studies. To a small extent girls in mixed-sex schools take more course work in mathematics. Chapter 4 shows that students in single-sex schools, especially girls, do considerably more homework than students in mixed-sex schools.

The adolescent subculture is strongest in male single-sex schools and weakest in female single-sex schools, with mixed-sex schools in between the other two types. In the minority sample, the specific figures on the adolescent subculture are as follows:

Male single-sex schools	61.39
Mixed-sex schools	53.00
Female single-sex schools	49.32

Because a strong adolescent subculture relates positively to boys' achievement and negatively to girls' achievement (see Figure 5.2), one would expect that these formal and informal structural differences between school types might account for some of the single-sex test score advantage.

For boys, the addition of all the school variables reduces the single-sex school advantage on each of the tests. For writing, science, and

TABLE 5.5. Adjusted Senior-Year Test Score Differences Between Minority Students in Predominantly Minority Mixed- and Single-Sex Catholic Schools (Expressed as a Percentage of One Grade Year Equivalent)

Curriculum-Specific Tests	Adjusted for Initial Ability and Home Background	(+)	Adjusted for Track[a] and Course work[b]	(+)	Adjusted for Homework[c]	(+)	Adjusted for Adolescent Context[d]
MALES							
Advanced Math	1.5*		1.4		1.3		0.8
Writing	0.8		0.8		0.7		-0.3
Science	0.3		0.1		0.1		-0.7
Civics	0.2		0.0		0.0		-0.2
FEMALES							
Advanced Math	-0.6		-1.0		-1.0		-1.3
Writing	0.3		0.3		0.2		0.2
Science	1.5*		1.6		1.8		1.7
Civics	1.9*		1.5		1.3		1.2

[a] Student-reported track placement as of the sophomore survey.

[b] This adjustment included course work in the specific test area, i.e., course work in math for the math test, course work in science for the science test, and so forth.

[c] Includes amount of homework per week reported in both the sophomore and senior years averaged as a single score.

[d] A variable aggregated to the school level based on "leading crowd" student responses regarding the extent of dating in the sophomore year, going steady or engaged in the sophomore year, attitudes toward students with good grades, and attitudes toward athletic students. A high score on this variable reflects a greater manifestation of the adolescent subculture.

* Sig. $p < 0.05$

civics, the school variables completely eliminate and reverse the test score advantage. Hence the combination of a college preparatory curriculum, demanding course work, homework, and a strong adolescent subculture "explains" why boys in single-sex schools outperform boys in mixed-sex schools on the writing, science, and civics tests. With regard to math, the school variables account for about 50 percent of the test score difference. Although each school variable does not influence each test score difference, each variable influences one test or another. Across all four tests, the school variables reduce the background-adjusted difference from an average of 0.7 to −0.1 of a grade year equivalent.

The results for girls are more complicated. Females in mixed-sex schools score higher on the advanced math test. The background-adjusted difference on this test is −0.6 (from Table 5.4), and it increases steadily to −1.3 as each school variable is added. The mixed-sex school advantage on this test is due to a series of factors. Hispanic females in mixed-sex schools score higher on the senior-year tests, although their initial sophomore scores are lower. Hispanic girls clearly gain more in advanced math from sophomore to senior year in mixed-sex schools. Black females in mixed-sex schools also gain slightly more on this test over the two-year period. This is a finding against single-sex schools; it is exacerbated in Table 5.5, which shows that the mixed-sex advantage would be even greater if these schools offered the type of curriculum, course work, homework, and climate provided in single-sex schools. If these students had access to the more favorable curriculum of students in single-sex schools, their test score advantage would have doubled (to 1.3). A large portion (0.7 of the 1.3) of the difference across school type is due to the formal and informal structure of single-sex schools. Thus, the structure of single-sex schools accounts for about 50 percent of an estimated test score difference that actually favors mixed-sex schools on this test.

The effect of the school variables on the other three tests for girls is straightforward. On the writing and civics tests, a reduction of 30 percent in the single-sex school advantage can be attributed to the school variables. On the science test, the overall influence of the school variables increases the single-sex advantage slightly. This is due largely to the fact that homework actually has a small negative effect on the senior science test score (among females only), thus favoring students in mixed-sex schools who do less homework. This finding duplicates an earlier one found among white girls in the regular school sample (see Table 5.3 and related discussion). Averaged across all four tests, the addition of the school variables reduces the background-adjusted difference from 0.8 to 0.5 of a grade equivalent, thus explaining more than one-third (38 percent) of the test score difference.

AFFECTIVE OUTCOMES

The primary objective of schooling is cognitive development. Secondarily, however, schools are concerned with the social and personal growth of students. Elementary schools, in fact, emphasize and grade students on a variety of deportment characteristics, and secondary schools continue this procedure to a lesser extent. It is expected that students will indicate growth with regard to personal responsibility, initiative, industriousness, cooperation, poise, and maturity. It is generally assumed, I think, that these outcomes are positively related to academic progress, as well as being independently meritorious.

The HSB survey provides data on certain affective outcomes, including self-esteem, sense of personal control, and a set of attitudinal questions on a variety of issues. One issue of particular interest is attitudes toward the idea of working women. Quite possibly, gender context may affect one or more of these attitudinal outcomes. If so, one would expect the results to parallel those obtained for cognitive outcomes. This is based on the assumption that higher academic achievement will be positively related to higher self-esteem, greater personal control over environmental forces, and a more liberal (educated) attitude towards the issue of working women. In addition, the overall climate of all-boys schools is less likely to produce positive attitudes toward women, whereas the climate at all-girls schools is likely to be very positive on this attitude.

In dealing with affective outcomes, however, it is important to realize that many factors other than schooling are known to be influential. Self-esteem and locus of control have been studied almost exhaustively. Such studies have found that factors such as race, social class, family structure, family size, birth order, and parental attitudes are related to both of these affective variables (Rosenberg, 1965; Rosenberg & Simmons, 1972). Hence, we would expect to find only moderate differences across school type on these affective outcomes, given the influence of home and family structure.

Self-esteem is viewed as liking and respecting oneself. It implies self-acceptance and a healthy, positive attitude toward one's own abilities and personal characteristics. There is little debate over whether it is better to have high or low self-esteem. Internal versus external locus of control refers to the extent to which people perceive that they have control over their actions and the consequences of those actions. People who believe they have some control over their destinies are called "internals"; that is, they believe that at least some control resides within themselves. "Externals," on the other hand, believe that the outcomes of their actions are determined by factors extrinsic to themselves — by fate, luck, or the "system."

Both self-esteem and locus of control have been shown to be positively related to academic achievement (Coleman et al., 1966; Rosenberg, 1965). Not surprisingly, minorities have been found consistently to be externally oriented. This seems to be a reasonable response to a subordinate situation in which one's life chances are often constrained by majority self-interest. With regard to blacks, research has shown that self-esteem decreases in racially integrated school settings, whereas levels of internal control increase (Coleman et al., 1966; Rosenberg & Simmons, 1972). In addition, Coleman and colleagues note that locus of control is, in fact, strongly related to black achievement. The loss of self-esteem has been attributed to the loss of a protected and insulated environment provided by black schools. The gain in control is undoubtedly caused by a far more encouraging and promising school environment. Relating this to gender context, one might expect that single-sex schools would have positive effects on locus of control, especially among minorities. Self-esteem may not be affected greatly, because there are forces pulling in many directions; that is, higher academic achievement may be offset by a problematic adolescent social life.

The self-esteem scale consists of four items, each with five response categories ranging from "disagree strongly" to "agree strongly." In one question, for example, students were asked: "I am able to do things as well as most other people." The locus of control scale also contains four items with the same format as the self-esteem scale. One example is: "Every time I try to get ahead, something or somebody stops me." Finally, attitudes toward working women are measured by three questions similar to the following: "Most women are happiest when they are making a home and caring for children." Each of these questions contains four categories ranging from "agree strongly" to "disagree strongly."

The analyses of these three attitudinal outcomes proceed in the same manner as for the cognitive results. I examine the senior-year differences in each attitude between students in single- and mixed-sex schools, separately for males and females in each sample. The raw difference is adjusted for initial attitude, initial ability, home background, and selected school variables. Unlike the cognitive test scores, however, it is not appropriate to convert the differences into grade equivalent values. Instead, the raw differences are converted into standard deviation units. In general, a difference of less than 0.2 of a standard deviation is not significantly different from zero, indicating no school effect. Table 5.6 displays the results of the analyses of these affective outcomes.

There are three central findings shown in Table 5.6. First, the effects of school type on these affective outcomes are generally small. None of the effects is greater than 0.3 of a standard deviation, and only 3 of the 12 separate effects are significant. Second, the school policy and adolescent subculture variables explain very little of whatever differences exist across the school types. In 7 of 12 effects, none of the difference is explained; in the others, the amount of difference that is accounted for is small. Third, there is a clear pattern to the data resembling the cognitive test score results. In the regular sample, boys in mixed-sex schools have higher self-esteem, higher internal control, and

TABLE 5.6. Adjusted Senior-Year Attitudinal Differences Between Students in Mixed- and Single-Sex Catholic Schools (Expressed as a Percentage of a Standard Deviation)

Criterion Variable	Males		Females	
	Adjusted for Initial Attitude, Initial Ability, and Home Background	Adjusted for Track, Homework, and Adolescent Subculture	Adjusted for Initial Attitude, Initial Ability, and Home Background	Adjusted for Initial Track, Homework, and Adolescent Subculture
White Students				
Self-Concept	-0.2	-0.1	0.0	0.0
Locus of Control	-0.1	-0.1	0.1	0.0
Attitudes Toward Working Women	-0.1	-0.1	0.2*	0.2*
Hispanic & Black Students				
Self-Concept	-0.1*	0.0*	0.0	0.1
Locus of Control	0.3*	0.3*	0.1	-0.1
Attitudes Toward Working Women	0.1	0.1	0.2*	0.2*

* Sig. p < 0.05

more liberal attitudes toward working women than do boys in single-sex schools. Girls in the regular sample and both boys and girls in the minority sample who are in single-sex schools generally score higher than their counterparts in mixed-sex schools. This finding corresponds to achievement differences found previously. One is led to conclude from this that white males attain healthier attitudinal outcomes in mixed-sex schools, whereas all other groups are better off in single-sex schools. Generally, however, the differences are not large.

Some additional findings turn up in Table 5.6. Girls in single-sex schools, not surprisingly, hold more liberal attitudes toward working women than girls in mixed-sex schools. Also, boys from single-sex schools in the minority sample have a significantly higher level of internal locus of control than boys in mixed-sex schools. It appears that for black and Hispanic males, single-sex schools provide an environment and a set of school policies which foster positive growth for internal locus of control. Conceivably, this affective outcome may, in turn, influence the higher academic achievement found among minority students in single-sex schools.

SUMMARY

In this chapter, we have examined the influence of single- and mixed-sex Catholic high schools on a set of cognitive and affective outcomes. To facilitate a summary of these cognitive measures, I have averaged the results from the four separate tests. Table 5.7 provides the average curriculum-specific test score differences by sex, sample type, and level of adjustment. Once again, it is imperative to separate the results by sample type. The regular Catholic school sample is a random data set generally representative of typical Catholic schools, which are predominantly white. The minority school sample, on the other hand, is a specially selected group of schools and students, and is *not* representative of Catholic secondary schools.

Outcomes in the Regular School Sample

After controlling for home background and initial ability, one finds that boys in single-sex schools score lower on the cognitive tests than boys in mixed-sex schools. Boys in single-sex schools begin with a number of substantial advantages. They come from homes of much higher socioeconomic status and from families with fewer children, and they have higher initial ability. The only possible negative background factor

TABLE 5.7. Average Adjusted Senior-Year Test Score
Difference by Sex, Sample Type, and Level of Adjustment
(Expressed as a Percentage of One Grade Year Equivalent)

	Adjusted for Ability and Background (Four Tests)	Adjusted for Ability and Background and School Variables (Four Tests)
Minority Sample		
Females	0.8	0.5
Males	0.7	-0.1
Regular Sample		
Females	0.5	0.3
Males	-0.1	-0.4

is that their mothers are more likely to have been employed during the school years. After adjusting for these differential background and initial ability factors, I found little difference in cognitive achievement, on average, between boys in single- and mixed-sex schools. Further adjustments for school variables (both formal and informal) indicate that boys currently in mixed-sex schools would score about one-half year grade equivalent (0.4) higher than boys in single-sex schools, if the various school factors were equivalent. The affective outcomes follow the same pattern. Boys in mixed-sex schools have higher self-esteem, higher sense of environmental control, and more egalitarian attitudes toward the role of women in society.

The results for girls, on the other hand, favor single-sex schools. Girls in single-sex schools differ little from girls in mixed-sex schools in either home background or initial ability. In fact, they come from homes of slightly lower socioeconomic status and are more likely to have an employed mother than are girls in mixed-sex schools. Yet, in our analyses of test scores, girls in single-sex schools show an average test score advantage of one-half year grade equivalent over girls in mixed-sex schools at the end of the senior year. Adjustments for home background and initial ability have no effect on the average grade equivalent advantage, although some decreases and increases occur in the individual tests. Lee and Bryk (1986) analyzed the same data using the pooled sample and achieved a greater degree of statistical significance on most of the measures reported here.

A small portion of this single-sex school advantage for girls derives from school policy variables. After adjusting for curriculum, course work, homework, and the adolescent subculture, the single-sex school advantage still averages 0.3 of a grade equivalent. Homework "explains" much more on the math test, accounting for 0.3 of a grade equivalent. Girls in single-sex schools do more homework than girls in mixed-sex schools, and in math it makes a substantial difference. Adjusting for differences in the adolescent subculture of the schools also decreases the single-sex school advantage for girls. In the final analysis, girls in single-sex schools score about one-third of a grade equivalent higher than girls in mixed-sex schools, on average. In science, this difference is almost one full year (0.9) of a grade equivalent advantage. These results are for a two-year period and would double over four years if things remained constant.

Outcomes in the Minority School Sample

In the minority school sample, both boys and girls (Hispanics and blacks) do better in single-sex schools. Among minority females, the average test score advantage of students in single-sex schools is 0.8 of a grade equivalent after controlling for initial ability and home background. For minority boys, the difference is 0.7. The initial raw differences increase slightly for boys in single-sex schools whose home background is slightly lower. Girls in single-sex schools, however, manifest higher initial abilities than girls in mixed-sex schools. Hence, among females the adjustment for initial ability decreases the raw uncontrolled differences.

One can explain about 70 percent of the test score difference in the minority school sample by adjusting for the set of school variables. Boys and girls are considerably advantaged in these formal and informal school structural components. Table 5.7 shows that after controls have been added for curriculum, course work, homework, and the adolescent subculture, the average test score difference is 0.5 for girls and −0.1 for boys, down from 0.8 and 0.7, respectively. In the case of males, the school variables explain 100 percent of the test score difference.

Both males and females gain something in terms of affective outcomes from being in single- rather than mixed-sex schools. Females in single-sex schools, not surprisingly, hold more egalitarian attitudes toward the role of women in society than do females in mixed-sex schools. (This sex-role attitude difference is true also for females in the regular school sample.) Black and Hispanic males in single-sex schools develop a greater sense of environmental control than do their counterparts in mixed-sex schools.

These then are the short-term results of single- and mixed-sex schooling for Catholic schools in the United States. Generally, educators and researchers have been satisfied with short-term outcomes. After all, schools cannot be held responsible for what happens to students after they graduate. Moreover, there are inherent difficulties in monitoring students' progress after they have left school. Finally, one might assume that the short-term effects would translate straightforwardly in the long run; that is, that successful students coming from good schools will go on to lead successful lives. The only problem with this taken-for-granted line of thinking is that very little is known regarding the enduring effects of education. Hence, we turn now to a close-order examination of the long-term effects of single- and mixed-sex schooling.

SIX

The Long-Term Effects
of Mixed- and
Single-Sex Schooling

It is commonly assumed that the cognitive, substantive, and affective outcomes of school remain as characteristics of individuals long after they have completed their formal schooling, or, at least, that those outcomes act as stepping-stones to role performance in adulthood. One reason for assuming that the effects of education are enduring is that educational attainment is directly related to occupational attainment. In their landmark study, Blau and Duncan (1967) demonstrated that the single most important determinant of occupational status was educational attainment. This has been widely replicated and taken by many to be, perhaps, one of the few unequivocal facts of social science. Thus, occupational achievement *is* a long-term effect of education in and of itself. Moreover, occupational prestige may be viewed as a measure of the cognitive complexity of occupations (Spaeth, 1976), and this is further evidence of the long-term effects of education. Duncan, Featherman, and Duncan (1972) report a correlation of .81 between occupational prestige and a scale of intelligence. Of course, some of this evidence may be spurious. Quite possibly, factors other than education (such as race, sex, and socioeconomic status) may be related to occupational achievement, and occupations themselves may either increase or decrease cognitive skills.

There is abundant evidence that the cognitive skills of students increase so long as they are in school. Contrary to the popular myth created as a reaction to the 1966 Coleman Report, schools *do* make a difference. However ineffective schooling may be, students increase their skills in all subject areas on an annual basis (see Coleman et al., 1966). Much less is known about the effects of schooling once the students are separated from their formal educational institutions.

This void of knowledge of long-term effects of schooling has several causes. There are obvious difficulties posed by studies that attempt to assess the long-term effects of education (Harnquist, 1977). The greatest obstacles are the problems associated with gathering longitudinal data on students after they have moved beyond their formal educational institutions. In fact, virtually all of the previous research has relied on zero-order correlations that have been pieced together by combining several different cross-sectional studies (Hyman, Wright, & Reed, 1975; Wolfle, 1980).

Of course, the matter becomes a bit more complicated if we undertake to study the long-term effects of different types of schools, which is what I propose to do here. To ask whether school makes a long-term difference is one thing. To ask whether different types of schools make a long-term difference requires an extra step. However, given the difficulties of assessing long-term effects, it is no added burden to control for school type. In this chapter, I present two analyses of the long-term effects of single- versus mixed-sex schooling. It is, to the best of my knowledge, the only such study available.*

Previous studies of long-term effects of schooling have been limited to (1) self-reported effects by alumni, (2) socioeconomic effects (occupational aspiration or achievement), and (3) surveys of public knowledge in cross-sectional sample surveys. Wolfle (1980) reviews studies in each of these areas. He reports that

> college graduates themselves feel as if the benefits derived from their education have persisted . . . the single most important causal determinant of occupational status . . . [is] educational attainment . . . [and on surveys of public knowledge] the higher the respondent's level of educational attainment the more often correct responses were given. (p. 105)

All of these studies are flawed either by self-selection, questionable measures of cognitive outcomes, and/or cross-sectional data.

Thus far, studies of the enduring effects of education have been limited to cognitive outcomes, occupational attainment, or satisfaction with schooling. Research on the endurance of affective outcomes has been omitted. In the area of immediate concern to us here, there is virtually no research whatsoever that examines the long-term effects of single- and mixed-sex schooling among secondary school graduates. Although some research does exist on college graduates of single- and

*As this book goes to press, Lee and Marks (1989) have just completed a preliminary study among 1982 high school graduates.

mixed-sex schools, it is almost entirely cross-sectional, anecdotal, self-reported, and/or devoid of important controls for initial ability and home background (for examples, see Oates & Williamson, 1980; Stoecker & Pascarella, 1988; Tidball, 1973, 1980). I intend this chapter to fill the void.

WOMEN'S COLLEGES

In the United States, the long-term effects of single- and mixed-sex colleges for women are of particular interest. Unlike primary and secondary schools, colleges and universities in America were largely single-sex institutions until the beginning of the twentieth century. Table 1.1 of Chapter 1 displays the growth of coeducation for selected years between 1870 and 1982. In 1870, the majority of colleges and universities were for men only (59%). By 1930, the majority of schools were coed (69%), and there were an equal number of male and female single-sex institutions. Since 1960, both men's and women's colleges have declined in number considerably. In 1960, there were 268 women's colleges in America; today only 100 are left. Presently, however, the remaining women's colleges may be enjoying "renewed vigor" (Ingalls, 1984; Sharp, 1979).

What the effects of single- and mixed-sex colleges for women are remains an unresolved empirical question. Of special interest are occupational choice and attainment, educational attainment, and marital outcomes, as well as cognitive and affective outcomes. Although studies have shown that students attending women's colleges have higher career aspirations and achievements, have lower dropout rates, and are more likely to enter graduate or professional schools (Astin, 1977; Tidball, 1973, 1980), some critics remain unconvinced (Oates & Williamson, 1978). A major problem with these studies has been a failure to control for "selection bias" and home background. That is, the superior achievements of alumnae from women's colleges may reflect only that prestigious women's colleges enroll women of superior academic ability who may have attended superior high schools. In addition to the absence of appropriate controls, most previous studies have been confined to non-random analyses of "successful" women who can be identified through biographical reference books, such as the Who's Who series. In this chapter I will examine the long-term effects of single- and mixed-sex colleges, while controlling for a variety of pertinent background and "selection bias" variables.

In all instances, the analyses of outcomes will control for both initial ability and home background. To control for these potentially confounding effects, the analyses rely on the statistical procedure of multiple regression. In this procedure, the effect of each predictor variable is computed under the statistical assumption that all students have similar levels of initial ability and home background. That is, the effects of school type are based on a standardization process that is built into the statistical calculations and that, in essence, equates respondents on other variables. In effect, I will *estimate* the educational, occupational, and attitudinal outcomes for students in both sectors that would be expected if each school type enrolled students of equivalent initial abilities, attitudes, and home backgrounds. This is the same procedure employed in Chapter 5, and the reader may once again find the Appendix to be helpful.

The Sample Data

The National Longitudinal Study of the High School Class of 1972 (NLS) is a longitudinal survey research project sponsored by the National Center for Education Statistics. The project employed a two-stage probability sample, with schools as first-stage sampling units and students as second-stage units. The base year questionnaire and a 69-minute test battery were administered in spring 1972 to 18,143 seniors who were enrolled in 1070 private, public, and church-affiliated secondary schools in the United States. Some schools were unable to participate during the base year, but were recontacted at the time of the first follow-up. The inclusion of some of these schools brought the data base to 22,652 students in 1318 schools. In addition to the student questionnaires, a variety of valuable data was gathered from school records. Follow-up surveys have been conducted in the years 1973, 1974, 1976, 1979, and 1986.

For each academic year from 1972–73 to 1978–79, the National Longitudinal Study obtained the name of each college attended by students in the survey. Each college is identified by a unique United States Department of Education vendor, or FICE, number. Drawing upon various sources, I compiled a list of women's colleges operating during 1972 to 1979.[1] Each women's college was identified according to its respective FICE code. Data on women attending a single-sex college during each academic year (1972–73 to 1978–79) were sorted and classified. In addition to the regular follow-up surveys, data were drawn also from the NLS Supplemental Survey of 1979.

A total of 198 women students were identified who had attended a single-sex college for at least one year during this seven-year period.

Fairly complete data were available for 180 of these 198 women. Of these, 123 attended a single-sex college for at least two years. Students who attended a single-sex college for only one year were eliminated from further consideration, since most of them would have a greater or equal number of years in a mixed-sex school. For analyses that include the 1986 data, only 92 of the 123 women were available.

Of the 123 women, 52 attended a single-sex school for at least four years and graduated. The NLS survey did not ask students to identify the college from which they graduated, although it would be possible to compute this through a complicated programming operation. For our purposes I assume that four years in a women's college plus college graduation equals graduation from a women's college. A separate analysis was conducted comparing these 52 college graduates with students of equivalent education from mixed-sex colleges ($N=2225$). For sections of the analyses dealing with the 1986 follow-up, complete data are available for only 39 of the 52 women. Although the sample size for women in single-sex colleges is small, the percentage (3 percent) in the single-sex sample is just about what one would expect. During the period from 1972 to 1979, single-sex colleges for women constituted 4 percent of all colleges and universities.

Variables

All measures used in the present study are obtained either from the student questionnaire, school records, or the test battery. Brief descriptions of the specific measures are provided below:

1. SES—a mean composite of five equally weighted standardized components: family yearly income, father's education, mother's education, father's occupation (using Duncan's occupational status scale), and household items (eight items)
2. COLLTYPE—college type (single- or mixed-sex); created as noted above
3. SAT—combination of verbal and mathematics scores on the College Board Examination
4. EDUC79—educational attainment as of 1979
5. EDUC86—educational attainment as of 1986
6. WORK79—work status in 1979 (full-time employment or other)
7. WORK86—work status in 1986 (full-time employment or other)
8. OCCUP79—Duncan's Socio-Economic Index (occupational prestige)

9. OCCUP86—Duncan's Socio-Economic Index (occupational prestige)

10. WOMROL76—1976 attitude toward the changing role of women; a total composite of the following attitudinal items with responses of "strongly agree" to "strongly disagree":

A working mother of preschool children can be just as good a mother as the woman who doesn't work.

It is usually better for everyone involved if the man is the achiever outside the home and the woman takes care of the children.

Most women are not interested in having big and important jobs.

Many qualified women can't get good jobs—men with the same skills have much less trouble.

High school counselors should urge young women to train for jobs that are now held mainly by men.

Men should be given first chance at most jobs because they have the primary responsibility.

11. WOMROL79—1979 attitude toward the changing role of women; a total composite of the above attitudes measured in the 1979 follow-up

12. SELF72—1972 attitude toward one's self; a composite of responses to the following four questions with responses ranging from "strongly agree" to "strongly disagree":

I take a positive attitude toward myself.

I feel I am a person of worth, on an equal plane with others.

I am able to do things as well as most other people.

On the whole, I'm satisfied with myself.

13. SELF86—1986 attitude toward self; a composite of responses to the four questions noted above during the 1986 follow-up

14. LOCUS72—1972 attitude toward control of one's own environment; a composite of responses to the following four questions with responses ranging from "strongly agree" to "strongly disagree":

Good luck is more important than hard work for success.

Every time I try to get ahead, something or somebody stops me.

Planning only makes a person unhappy since plans hardly ever work out anyway.

People who accept their condition in life are happier than those who try to change things.

15. LOCUS86—1986 attitude toward control of one's own environment; a composite of responses to the four questions noted above during the 1986 follow-up

16. HAPMAR—1986 degree of marital happiness; a composite of six questions, each of which asked respondents how happy they were during the first, second, third, fourth, fifth, and most recent year of mar-

riage. The range of responses to each question were (7) extremely happy
to (1) extremely unhappy. A high score indicates greater happiness.

Students with Two or More Years of College

I begin by considering those women in the sample who completed
at least two years of college. Table 6.1 displays the bivariate relationship
of college type to educational and occupational attainment, parental
socioeconomic status and SAT scores, and several other interesting long-
term outcomes. SAT scores were used in lieu of scores from the NLS test
battery to reduce the loss of cases due to missing data. Students who
attended single-sex colleges (for at least two years) attain higher levels

TABLE 6.1. College Type by Selected Variables
for Women Only[a]

Selected Variables	Single Sex College[b]	Mixed Sex College
Background (1972)		
Parental socioeconomic status		
(mean = 0)	.41	.19**
Combined SAT score	997	949*
Status Attainment (1986)		
Educational attainment (in years)	16.4	15.5**
% college graduates	88%	48%**
Occupational prestige		
(scale of 0–100)	67.9	56.9**
Spouse's occupational prestige		
(scale of 0–100)	59.3	56.5
Affective Outcomes (1986)		
Self-esteem (scale of 1–5)	4.5	4.3*
Locus of control (scale of 1–5)	4.3	4.1*
Marital Outcomes (1986)		
% still with first partner	82%	65%**
% two or more marriages	7%	16%**
Marital happiness (scale of 6–42)	36.0	34.0*

* $p < .05$, using a two-tailed test.

* $p < .003$, using a two-tailed test.

[a] Includes only students who attained at least two years of college.

[b] Includes only students who attended a single-sex school for two years or more.

of educational attainment than students who attended mixed-sex colleges. Nearly 90 percent of the women who attended a single-sex college graduated from college, compared with 50 percent of women from mixed-sex colleges. Students from single-sex colleges also achieved higher occupational status than students from mixed-sex schools, and interestingly enough, so did their spouses.

Table 6.1 suggests that there are additional differences among women in single- and mixed-sex colleges. Women who attended a single-sex college for at least two years have higher self-esteem and a higher sense of control of their own environment than do their counterparts who attended mixed-sex colleges. Also, women from coeducational institutions are more likely to have been divorced and unhappy in their marriages than students attending women's colleges.

In Table 6.1, all of the relationships, except spouse's occupation, are significant below .05. Moreover, the differences in unstandardized terms are striking—.9 of a year of education, 11 units on the occupational prestige scale (on a scale that ranges from 0 to 100), and a 17 percentage point gap in marital stability. In fact, the educational, occupational, and marital differences are highly significant ($p < .003$). These educational and occupational advantages exist as early as 1979, but are not as large as shown in Table 6.1 for 1986. The self-esteem and self-control variables are also strongly related to school type ($p < .03$).

Table 6.1 also shows that college type is related to both socioeconomic status and SAT score. Students who attended single-sex colleges had higher initial cognitive ability and came from homes of higher socioeconomic status than did students who attended mixed-sex schools. Both of these variables are antecedent to college type and each represents a potential common cause of the relationship between college type and educational or occupational achievement. Although not shown in Table 6.1, both parental socioeconomic status (SES) and SAT are strongly related to both educational and occupational achievement.[2] Thus, Table 6.1 suggests that women attain greater achievements in single-sex colleges, but that these achievements may be due to factors that are antecedent to college type; namely, higher cognitive ability and an advantaged home background. This issue can be resolved by a multivariable regression analysis.

The model to be tested is shown in Figure 6.1. The model and the analysis are rather elementary. If socioeconomic status and/or SAT ability are common causes, the relationship between college type and educational or occupational achievement should be significantly reduced. In the regression analysis of educational attainment on college type, we control for SES and SAT scores simultaneously. In the regression of occu-

FIGURE 6.1. Model of Educational and Occupational Attainment

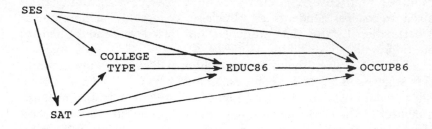

pational achievement on college type, work status and education are also added as controls. It is, however, unnecessary to control for work status, because an equal proportion (75 percent) of women from each school type were in the work force in 1986. The results of this analysis are shown in Table 6.2.

Educational and Occupational Attainment

Beginning with educational attainment, we note that the unstandardized, unadjusted effect of college type is .85 of a year of education. This is the educational attainment difference (.9) between students in single- and mixed-sex colleges as shown in Table 6.1. In this and all the regression analyses that follow, the unstandardized regression coefficient represents the average difference between students in single- and mixed-sex schools on the specific dependent variable. A positive value means that students in single-sex schools score higher; a negative value

TABLE 6.2. Unstandardized Regression Effects of College Type on Educational Attainment and Occupational Prestige for Women

Dependent Variable	Unadjusted Effect	Adjusted for			
		SES	SAT	EDUC86	WORK86
EDUC86[*]	.85	.72	.63	--	--
OCCUP86[*]	10.53	9.94	9.49	6.84	6.80

[*] All coefficients are significant at p < .03, using two-tailed tests.

favors students in mixed-sex schools. Adjusting for socioeconomic home background and initial cognitive ability reduces the direct effect of college type on educational attainment to .63 (three-fifths of a year of education). Most important, following the adjustment the effect of college type remains significantly greater than zero. This suggests that the relationship of college type to educational attainment is *not* spurious.

The results for occupational attainment parallel those for education. The unadjusted effect of college type on occupational prestige is 10.53 (on a scale of 0 to 100). After the appropriate control variables are added, this difference is understandably reduced, but remains clearly and substantially significant. Among women of equivalent home background, initial cognitive ability, educational attainment, and work status, students from women's colleges score 6.80 occupational prestige units higher than their counterparts from mixed-sex colleges. Attending a women's college for two or more years increases eventual educational and occupational attainment.

One might suppose that the women's colleges in our sample are mostly elite "Ivy League" schools. The parental socioeconomic status and SAT scores suggest that the women attending single-sex colleges are a notch above average. In fact, however, the composition of the list of women's colleges is very broad, representing, as it should, the full array of these schools. Of those students in the above analysis who attended a single-sex school for two or more years, about 10 percent attended one of the "Seven Sisters" schools, an additional 20 percent attended high-quality, four-year schools, and the remainder attended lesser known Catholic, public, and private schools, and junior colleges. This breakdown holds also for the analysis of women college graduates which follows below. Thus, the elite institutions are *not* overrepresented in the sample. Moreover, by controlling for home background and SAT scores, we approximate a control for the status of the college as well.

Self-Esteem, Locus of Control, and Marital Happiness

In order to further examine some of the affective outcomes, I conducted a similar regression analysis for the variables of self-esteem, locus of control, and marital happiness. The results are shown in Table 6.3. Unlike educational and occupational achievement, the affective outcomes turn out technically to be spurious correlations. When parental background and precollege cognitive ability (SAT) are controlled, the effect of college type on these affective outcomes is reduced to a point below standard levels of statistical significance. If we allow for a one-tailed test and a probability of .07, however, women from single-sex

TABLE 6.3. Unstandardized Regression Effects of College
Type on Marital Happiness, Self-Esteem, and
Locus of Control for Women

Dependent Variable	Unadjusted Effect	Adjusted for			
		SES	SAT	72ATTITUDE	EDUC86
HAPMAR	2.20	2.05	2.07	----	1.73
SELF86	.17*	.17*	.17*	.14*	.12
LOCUS86	.17*	.15*	.13*	.11	.09

* p < .07, using a one-tailed test.

colleges do manifest higher levels of self-esteem than women from
mixed-sex schools. (A one-tailed test can be justified under the assumption that women attending single-sex schools will actually score higher
than women from mixed-sex schools. The two-tailed probability is .14.)
This is true even after controlling for initial 1972 levels of self-esteem.
The same finding holds to a lesser extent for locus of control. The
pattern of the data is clearly in the direction of single-sex schools, even
regarding marital happiness.

In Chapter 3 we pointed out arguments in favor of mixed-sex
schools, which maintain that they offer an environment more conducive to self-development and personal happiness than that in single-sex
schools. Proponents of single-sex schools, on the other hand, maintain
that they provide an environment conducive to learning. Despite the
lack of standard statistical significance, Table 6.3 suggests that women
attending single-sex colleges will fare no worse in terms of marital happiness and self-development, and will probably be better off. This, of
course, applies only to women and women's colleges.

College Graduates

It might be argued that the above analyses are less than fair tests of
the effectiveness of single-sex colleges. Of the 92 women in these analyses, only 39 actually graduated from a single-sex college. The others
attended a single-sex college for two or three years. Some of these
women either did not graduate from any college or attended a single-sex
college for only two years. In either case, the full probative effects of a

single-sex college are constrained. Consequently, I conducted an analysis of the 39 graduates of women's colleges compared with women graduates of mixed-sex colleges ($N=2091$).

In this analysis, problems arise due to the small number of women's college respondents in the sample. Quite surprisingly, the ultimate educational attainment by graduates of women's colleges is slightly *lower* than that of women graduates of mixed-sex colleges. It appears that having attained a baccalaureate degree, graduates of women's colleges are less likely to pursue an advanced degree than are graduates of coeducational schools. The relationship of this finding to other outcomes is somewhat elusive; it is suggested but not fully revealed in the analysis of the 1986 data. Specifically, graduates of women's colleges are more likely to remain at home in the early years following graduation than are graduates of coeducational schools. However, this does not show up in the 1986 data, which show graduates of both school types equally likely to be employed. Therefore, to increase the case base and further pursue the puzzle, I conducted an analysis of college graduates using the 1979 data. This turns out to have one additional advantage; namely, the 1979 data include a set of items measuring attitudes toward the changing role of women.

Table 6.4 displays the results of a regression of educational and occupational achievement on college type for students who were college graduates in 1979. The results are interesting and complex. Unlike the earlier analysis, we find here that women from mixed-sex colleges are significantly more likely than those from single-sex colleges to obtain a graduate degree. This result reverses a pattern favoring single-sex colleges in Table 6.2 and holds after controlling for home background and initial SAT ability. Apparently, single-sex undergraduate education is not

TABLE 6.4. Unstandardized Regression Effects of College Type on Educational and Occupational Attainment for Women College Graduates

Dependent Variable	Unadjusted Effect	Adjusted for			
		SES	SAT	EDUC79	WORK79
EDUC79	-.20	-.21	-.27*	--	--
OCCUP79	2.70	2.51	1.77	2.93	3.97

* p < .05, using a two-tailed test.

especially conducive to further schooling. This may also reflect the fact that (in 1979) graduates of women's colleges expected to have more children and were less likely to be employed full-time than graduates of mixed-sex colleges.

Despite having actually achieved less education, however, graduates of women's colleges are more likely to hold a higher-prestige job than their counterparts from mixed-sex colleges. This difference in occupational prestige is decreased when adjustments are made for home background and initial ability, indicating once again that at least part of the effect of college type is spurious. When controls are added for educational attainment and work status, however, the effect is actually increased.

Among students with equivalent cognitive ability, home background, and educational attainment, graduates of women's colleges score three occupational prestige units higher than women from mixed-sex colleges. Considering that their educational attainment is lower on average, graduates of women's colleges appear to get more occupational mileage from each year of education than women from mixed-sex colleges. This finding hints at possible differences in educational quality between single- and mixed-sex colleges, and/or motivational factors that might also be attributed to school type. When a final adjustment is made for work status, the difference in occupational achievement increases to four units. Graduates of women's colleges are slightly less likely to work full-time than women graduates of mixed-sex colleges. The final difference is still insignificant ($p < .07$, using a one-tailed test), but it is not small.

Graduates of women's colleges are more likely to remain at home after obtaining a baccalaureate degree than are women graduates of mixed-sex colleges. Women from single-sex colleges also expect to have larger families than women from mixed-sex colleges. (This probably reflects the fact that many women's colleges are Catholic institutions.) For this reason, women from single-sex colleges are less likely to obtain an advanced degree. Nonetheless, they still manage to achieve higher-prestige jobs, especially when educational attainment and work status are held constant.

Other Outcomes

It is interesting to note that graduates of women's colleges are more likely to marry men of higher occupational prestige than are graduates of mixed-sex colleges, even after controlling for home background and initial ability. This finding is true for both college graduates and those with two or more years of college, and in both 1979 and 1986. It holds for the variable of the men's income as well as occupational prestige. What would account for the greater occupational success of these men? Why are they more likely to be married to women from single-sex colleges? How is the success of the husbands related to the success of their wives? Is it possibly a case of the old cliché that "behind every great man is a great woman"? Or, more relevant here perhaps, do successful husbands facilitate occupational success for their wives? Or, is it the case that women's colleges are more likely to foster an "MRS." mentality, leading their students to place a higher value on marriage than students do in coeducational schools? Answers to these questions are not readily available in the NLS data or elsewhere.

A set of items in the survey, however, does measure attitudes toward the changing role of women. These questions were asked of respondents in both 1976 and 1979. Six of the items were combined to form a composite measure. A high score on this measure indicates a strong egalitarian attitude toward the educational and occupational roles of women and men. As with educational and occupational achievement, I analyzed the attitudinal results for women who had completed two or more years of college separately from those women who were college graduates. Among students with only two or more years of college, I found no effect for college type on attitudes toward an egalitarian role for women. Quite possibly, for certain hard-to-change attitudes, a four-year, single-sex college education may be necessary to make a real difference.

Among college graduates, however, the effect of college type on these attitudes is substantial. Considering the 1976 results first, Table 6.5 shows that graduates of women's colleges are significantly more positive or enthusiastic with regard to the changing role of women than are graduates of mixed-sex colleges. (Recall that a positive value indicates that students in single-sex schools score higher than students in mixed-sex schools.) The effect is reduced only slightly when controls are added for socioeconomic status, SAT score, and educational attainment as of 1976.

By 1979, the difference between graduates of single- and mixed-sex colleges has lessened (as we would expect) but is still significant and strong. This direct effect is greatly reduced when WOMROL76 is added to the regression equation. The initial measure of this attitude is by far the strongest predictor of the later measure. College type, however, is a strong predictor of the initial attitude. Hence, although the direct

TABLE 6.5. Unstandardized Regression Effects of College
Type on Attitudes Toward the Changing Role of Women
Among Women College Graduates

| | | | Adjusted for | | | EDUC79, OCCUP79, |
Dependent Variable	Unadjusted Effect	SES	SAT	EDUC76	WOMROL76	WORK79
WOMROL76	1.41*	1.40*	1.18*	1.22*	--	--
WOMROL79	1.05*	1.00	.82	--	.12	.21

* p < .05, using a two-tailed test.

effect of college type on WOMROL79 is low, the indirect effect through
WOMROL76 is high. Specifically, the controlled direct effect of WOMROL76
on WOMROL79 is .58 (not shown in Table 6.5). The indirect effect of
college type on WOMROL79 through WOMROL76 is .71 (1.22×.58). This
indirect effect of college type plus the controlled direct effect (.21 from
Table 6.5) equals .92, which is almost equivalent to the unadjusted zero-
order effect. This logic is shown in Figure 6.2.

All in all, the data suggest that graduates of women's colleges are
more positively oriented to a more equitable role for women than are
graduates of mixed-sex colleges. This attitude is established during college or upon graduation (1976); it, in turn, continues to influence later
attitudes (1979). Stated differently, one's attitude toward the changing
role of women is established initially and significantly by college type,
and eventually it "explains" and/or "mediates" the influence of college
type on the later manifestation of the same attitudes.

FIGURE 6.2. Direct and Indirect Effect of College
Type on Attitudes Toward Equal Sex Roles

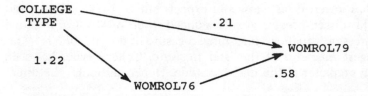

CATHOLIC HIGH SCHOOLS

In Chapter 5, we examined the short-term outcomes of single- and mixed-sex Catholic secondary schools. I want to return to these schools here and take a look at their long-term results. In Chapter 5, we relied on the High School and Beyond (HSB) survey, which began in 1980 with measures of high school sophomores. In that earlier analysis, I compared the effects of single- and mixed-sex Catholic schooling for a set of senior-year measures—test scores and affective outcomes. All of these were short-term results as of 1982. Although data are available for these students for 1984 and 1986, they are still relatively limited.* Certainly, it would be premature to assess occupational achievement for these students; in fact, as of 1986, many of them had not even completed their eventual educational attainment. Hence, I turn again to the NLS data described earlier in this chapter.

The data collected in the HSB study were designed in part to replicate the National Longitudinal Study of the High School Class of 1972 (Heynes & Hilton, 1982). The NLS survey is particularly useful for determining long-term outcomes, because data are available for students 14 years out of high school and 7 to 10 years out of college. The NLS data contain a sample of single- and mixed-sex Catholic high schools. Unlike the HSB survey, however, the NLS data contain mostly white students from predominantly white schools. Therefore, the following analysis is confined to white students only. As in Chapter 5, the gender context of each school was determined by examining the male–female ratio in each school.

I use the same variables here as noted earlier in the study of women's and coeducational colleges. Again, I will examine long-term outcomes for both 1979 and 1986. In this case, however, the results are presented for males and females separately, as was done in Chapter 5. Three additional variables will be considered here. In the 1979 followup, measures were obtained for both mathematical and verbal ability; these two tests allow for an analysis of long-term cognitive outcomes. Unfortunately, the tests were given only to a small subsample of respondents in the 1979 survey. This greatly reduces the case base for these tests and, in fact, prohibited their use in the earlier analysis of mixed- and single-sex colleges (because there were so few people from single-sex colleges to begin with). For each of the four sex-by-school type categories shown in Table 6.6, there are generally 150 to 250 respon-

---

*Lee and Marks (1989) have reported some preliminary results for these HSB students in terms of attitudes and values.

TABLE 6.6.   High School Type by Selected Variables[a]

Selected Variables	Boys		Girls	
	Single	Mixed	Single	Mixed
Background (1972)				
Parental socioeconomic status	.36	.20**	.09	.06
Cognitive ability (verb+math)	167	164	166	162*
Various Outcomes (1979)				
Verbal ability (0-15)	11.6	11.9	12.1	9.6**
Mathematical ability (0-25)	16.8	18.0	15.3	10.8**
Educational attainment (years)	14.9	14.3**	14.0	13.7*
Occupational prestige (0-100)	55.4	48.0**	52.9	52.0
Role of women (4-16)	13.6	13.9	14.7	14.6
Status Attainment (1986)				
Educational attainment	16.2	16.0	15.6	15.4
Occupational prestige	59.7	58.3	55.1	53.8
Affective Outcomes (1986)				
Self-esteem (1-5)	4.4	4.4	4.3	4.2
Locus of control (1-5)	4.2	4.1	4.1	4.1
Marital Outcomes (1986)				
% still with first partner	75%	80%	75%	72%
% two or more marriages	12%	6%	8%	10%
Marital happiness (6-42)	36.4	35.6	33.7	34.9

[a] For each of the four sex-by-school type categories shown, there are generally 150 to 250 respondents. There are more people available for 1979 than for 1986. For the 1979 measures of cognitive ability the case base is reduced drastically and ranges from 26 to 41 in each category. The variable of marital happiness also contains fewer respondents (75-100).

* p < .05, using a two-tailed test.

** p < .01, using a two-tailed test.

dents. There are more people available for 1979 than for 1986. For the 1979 measures of cognitive ability, the case base is reduced drastically and ranges from 26 to 41 in each category. In addition to these 1979 tests, I use a combined verbal and mathematical composite to measure the students' 1972 senior-year cognitive ability.

Table 6.6 displays the overall long-term effects of high school type on a variety of outcome variables. Also shown in Table 6.6 are estimates of parental socioeconomic status and senior-year cognitive ability. As we found in Chapter 4, males in single-sex schools come from homes of significantly higher social class than males attending mixed-sex schools. Some part, therefore, of any outcome advantage favoring single-sex schools for boys must be due to their having been raised in more advantaged homes.

The socioeconomic home background of girls, on the other hand, is not significantly different according to school type. Girls in single-sex schools, however, manifest higher cognitive ability than their counterparts in mixed-sex schools. It seems likely that this short-term cognitive outcome can be attributed to differences in the gender context of the schools. It is not possible to test this assertion conclusively, however, because the NLS data did not provide measures of earlier initial ability (as did the HSB survey—see Chapter 5). We can, however, control for home background. Table 6.7 indicates that the school type difference in senior-year cognitive ability among girls remains significant even after controlling for parental socioeconomic status. This finding is entirely consistent with the results reported in Chapter 5, using the more rigorous controls available in the HSB survey. (For a more extensive analysis of these 1972 NLS cognitive outcomes, see Riordan, 1985.)

Turning first to the 1979 outcomes, we note in Table 6.6 that the

TABLE 6.7. Unstandardized Regression Effects of High School Type on Cognitive Ability, Educational and Occupational Attainment

Dependent Variable	Unadjusted Effect	Adjusted for		
		SES	ABILITY	EDUC79
BOYS				
ABILITY72	3.47	1.94	----	----
VERB79	-0.34	-0.42	-0.50	-0.53
MATH79	-1.15	-1.53	-1.74	-2.05*
EDUC79	0.53**	0.35*	0.31	----
OCCUP79	7.37**	6.23**	5.96**	4.23*
GIRLS				
ABILITY72	4.17*	4.04*	----	----
VERB79	2.56**	2.57**	2.28**	2.15**
MATH79	4.48**	4.45**	3.78**	3.65**
EDUC79	0.33*	0.31	0.19	----
OCCUP79	0.90	0.84	0.41	-0.04

* $p < .05$, using a two-tailed test.

** $p < .01$, using a two-tailed test.

1972 difference in cognitive ability persists until 1979. Girls from single-sex Catholic high schools manifest significantly higher verbal and mathematical ability than their counterparts from mixed-sex schools, fully seven years after graduation. Since some of this 1979 difference might be due to the initial school effect from 1972 or to a difference in educational attainment, I conducted a regression analysis on these variables, holding 1972 ability and 1979 education constant. The results, shown in Table 6.7, indicate that a very strong single-sex high school effect remains for girls in terms of both mathematical and verbal ability.

Although it may appear that boys in single-sex schools have higher cognitive ability as seniors in 1972 (see Table 6.6), this nonsignificant difference is cut in half when appropriate controls are added for home socioeconomic background, as shown in Table 6.7. By 1979, boys from mixed-sex schools demonstrate higher ability than boys from single-sex schools in both mathematical and verbal skills. Although these findings are not significant in Table 6.6, they become significant when controls are added for home background and 1972 cognitive ability, as shown in Table 6.7. These results confirm those of Chapter 5. At least in terms of cognitive outcomes, white males do better in mixed-sex schools.

With regard to educational and occupational achievement, however, boys from single-sex schools attained more education and higher occupational status than boys who graduated from mixed-sex Catholic schools. These advantages remain even after controlling for the appropriate background and intervening variables, as shown in Table 6.7. It may be, however, that the difference in educational attainment is due in large part to initial differences in home background. Table 6.7 shows that the educational effect becomes almost insignificant when socioeconomic status is controlled. It is quite possible that boys from single-sex schools achieve more education mostly because of the influence of home background (rather than because of better schooling). From that point on, their education carries them on to higher occupational achievement. Among girls, there is a small educational difference favoring those who graduated from a single-sex school, but no effect for occupational achievement. There are no long-term school effects regarding attitudes toward equal roles for women and men, or with regard to any of the other attitudinal outcomes. It is useful to repeat, however, that we did find short-term positive results for girls in single-sex schools on the equal-sex-role variable (see Affective Outcomes, Chapter 5), and that the initial outcome on this variable is the strongest predictor of the later attitude (see Figure 6.2).

It appears that the enduring effects of school type are not boundless. None of the 1986 outcomes shown in Table 6.6 are significant, nor are they large in any sense. Although there still are educational and occupational differences favoring single-sex schools, it is clear that the major influence of school type has already occurred. This is as it should be. The further removed one is from the source of influence, the weaker the relationship. It is important to note that the null findings with regard to affective and marital outcomes are yet another strike against mixed-sex schools. According to their proponents, mixed-sex schools ought to provide, at a minimum, a more natural environment conducive to more positive self-development and personal happiness. Judging from these data, they do not do this.

SUMMARY

In this chapter, I have conducted a close-order examination of the long-term effects of single- and mixed-sex schooling. To accomplish this, I have drawn upon data from the National Longitudinal Study of the High School Class of 1972, which provides follow-up data for these 1972 high school seniors through 1986, fully 14 years beyond high school. First, I compared a group of women from this sample who attended single-sex colleges with their counterparts who attended mixed-sex colleges. Then I compared those students who attended single- or mixed-sex Catholic high schools. For each comparison, I used a variety of long-term measures, including cognitive and affective outcomes, educational and occupational attainment, and attitudes toward the changing role of women in modern society.

Once again, as in Chapter 5, the results favor single-sex schools for women. With regard to the college-level results, there are clearly *no* negative affective or attitudinal outcomes for women attending single-sex schools. In fact, these women hold much stronger views toward equal sex roles than women graduates of mixed-sex colleges. Similarly, students from women's colleges manifest higher levels of self-esteem, self-control, and marital happiness than women from coeducational institutions. These latter differences are not statistically significant (at standard levels), but the pattern of the data is consistently in favor of single-sex colleges. These findings are particularly important because they contradict one of the main rationales offered by proponents of mixed-sex schools—that mixed-sex schools provide a better environment for personal growth and happiness.

In addition to these affective outcomes, women's colleges have a very strong influence on both educational and occupational achievement. Considering those students who attended a women's college for at least two years, I found that they obtain significantly more education and occupational prestige than comparable students who attended only mixed-sex colleges. These results hold even after controls have been made to allow for initial differences in home background and ability.

However, women who graduate from a single-sex college are significantly less likely to obtain advanced education than women who graduate from a coeducational college. This appears to be due to the fact that they are less likely to work full-time in the early years following graduation and they plan to have more children than do women from mixed-sex colleges. Nonetheless, the occupational attainments of women's college graduates are higher than those of women graduates of mixed-sex colleges.

The long-term high school effects also favor single-sex schools for women. Just as in Chapter 5, we found in the analysis of the NLS data that girls in single-sex high schools outperform girls attending mixed-sex schools in cognitive ability. This difference appears first in the senior-year measures and persists seven years later. The difference holds even after controlling for home background, initial (1972) ability, and 1979 educational attainment, and it is significant despite the small sample size. Not surprisingly, in the 1979 follow-up, girls from single-sex high schools had also achieved higher education than their female counterparts from mixed-sex high schools.

The long-term effects also favor boys from single-sex schools insofar as educational and occupational achievement are concerned. This is true despite any difference in cognitive outcomes across the two school types in either the long or short term. In fact, after our controlling for initial ability and home background, the 1979 cognitive outcomes actually favor boys from mixed-sex schools. Similarly, in Chapter 5 we found no short-term cognitive advantages for white males in single-sex schools, and the long-term results for high school students apply only to whites. Hence, the educational and occupational advantages for boys from single-sex high schools may represent the influence of an advantaged home rather than better schooling.

The enduring effects of school type diminish over time. This is neither surprising nor troublesome. By 1986, no significant differences exist between students who graduated from single- and mixed-sex high schools in 1972. But the influence of school type persists in 1986 in the form of indirect effects.

SEVEN

Reconsidering
Single-Sex
Education

Over the past century, American education has wrestled with duplicity. Ever since the Committee of Ten (National Education Association, 1893) advocated a more demanding classical education for all students, a variety of social forces have acted to ensure that the reality of schooling remains patently anti-intellectual. Powell, Farrar, and Cohen (1985) document this process in *The Shopping Mall High School.* They show how high school attendance expanded at the turn of the twentieth century largely because of economic and technological changes, *not* because of a youthful hunger for academic learning.

Mass schooling was created as a result of a reduced need for adolescents to work. In 1900, only 11 percent of American high school-aged youth were in high school; by 1930, the figure jumped to 70 percent (Trow, 1961); today, it is over 90 percent. Child labor and compulsory attendance laws stimulated this growth, as did major transformations that occurred in the economy, the family, and the household. As Coleman (1987) notes, the expansion of schooling was accompanied and perhaps precipitated by a shift of the dominant work locations of men and women from the household to the corporation, office, or factory. This implies that from the turn of the century onward, increasing numbers of young people attended schools. Displaced from the labor force and facing empty homes, adolescents turned to each other.

Historically, therefore, students rarely attended schools primarily for educational benefits and opportunities. Rather, as the Lynds (1929) and Hollingshead (1949) observed from their community studies, extracurricular activities, sports, and socializing were the primary attractions. Schools, in effect, created the adolescent subculture. "Most students seemed not to have wanted a heavy academic diet, and in general they got what they wanted" (Powell et al., 1985, p. 239). Powerless to do otherwise, teachers reluctantly adjusted to this state of affairs in the form of "bargains" and "treaties" that are worked out with students in the classroom, leading at best to a mediocre system of education.

Perhaps there was a time when the goals of educators were congruent with the goals of parents and students; perhaps there was not. At any rate, over the past century we have witnessed something less than a golden age of schooling (Powell et al., 1985; Sedlak et al., 1986). During this time, educators have assumed that their major objective was academic learning; students have assumed otherwise. This seemingly bold conclusion is well founded, though not openly acknowledged. Goodlad (1984, p. 39), for example, found that high school teachers were twice as likely as their students to prefer intellectual goals over social, personal, and vocational goals. He also reports that parents are at least reasonably satisfied with the schools just as they are.

Educators have consistently regarded the schools as substandard. The report by the Twentieth Century Fund (1983) unabashedly asserted: "By almost every measure—the commitment and competency of teachers, student test scores, truancy and dropout rates, crimes of violence—the performance of our schools falls far short of our expectations" (p. 3). This view is shared by more than 30 commissions, task forces, and individuals who produced reports on the state of American education since 1980. These critiques identify the absence of academic excellence and productivity as the central problem facing American education today. Over the past 25 years, measured teacher satisfaction has exhibited an alarming drop. According to membership polls conducted every five years by the National Education Association, 50 percent of all teachers in 1961 said they would certainly choose to become teachers if they had to do it again; by 1986, the figure had decreased to 23 percent (Webb & Sherman, 1989, p. 203). Such dissatisfaction has stimulated numerous proposals at the national, state, and local levels for enhancing academic standards in the schools. Yet by most accounts little progress or change has occurred.

ORGANIZATIONAL STRUCTURES AND SCHOOL REFORM STRATEGIES

What accounts for this inability of the schools to move forward, to change, to reform? After all, other large institutions have "modernized" over the years. Bureaucratized as it is, even the Catholic Church has undertaken major reforms. In education, however, the history of reform is mostly a set of commission reports gathering dust. In fact, with few exceptions (common school, progressive education, comprehensive high school), virtually every change in education can be traced to government intervention in the form of laws or subsidies or to parental and student revolt. Part of the problem, I believe, lies in a failure to recognize and account for the fundamental and unique duplicity of goals, which I have identified above. Unlike the professions of law and medicine, where clients and professionals share the same goals, professional educators and their clients are at odds with one another. Moreover, organizational change or reform requires an accurate conception of the organization. However, the school as reformers often conceive it no longer corresponds to the school as it now exists (perhaps it never did).

In the face of the recurrent failures of reform, scholars share a growing sense that the problems of education extend beyond the schools. Over the past decade, an array of social conditions circumscribing the schools and acting as obstacles to school improvement have been identified. Taken together, Goodlad (1984) and Coleman (1987) pinpoint the following conditions:

1. A growing proportion of employed mothers
2. A growing proportion of single-parent families
3. Increases in the percentage of families broken by divorce
4. Increases in the percentage of households without children
5. Decreases in the percentage of adults populating family units, i.e., a sharp decline of the extended family
6. Decreases in church attendance and membership
7. Decreases in the solidarity of communities or neighborhoods
8. Fewer coalitions of legislators, parents, school board members, school administrators, teachers, business leaders, and others
9. An increasingly segmented educational profession
10. An increasing diversity of students in the schools
11. The increasing role and impact of television

These social transformations, however accountable they may be for impeding school reform, cannot account for the failure of schools to clearly define their organizational structure and processes.

John Goodlad (1984) makes the point "that the didactics of the classroom can be—and indeed are—very much the same from school-to-school and yet often are presented within a context of considerable school-to-school difference in the eyes of principals, teachers, students, and parents" (p. 247). In *A Place Called School*, Goodlad demonstrates that schools are really very much alike, especially with regard to those things commonly regarded as unique to schooling—namely, "the mechanics of teaching, the kinds of activities in which students are engaged in classrooms, the modes of learning encouraged, instructional materials, tests and quizzes, grouping practices, and classroom management" (p. 246).

Thus, those aspects of schooling that most distinguish it from other institutions *do not* differ significantly from school to school. Rather, it is those characteristics of schooling that are shared by other types of organizations and institutions (such as business, industry, government, the military) that often differ from school to school. Goodlad notes these latter school characteristics (such as school size, sex ratio, orientation to academic concerns, informal or adolescent norms, relationship between teachers and principal) are less likely to be experienced by visitors and observers (that is, researchers). Understandably then, the real structural differences that exist between schools have often been overlooked.

If some schools are more effective than others and if schools do not differ significantly in their curricula and instructional practices, then the differential outcomes must derive from structural differences that schools share with all other organizations and institutions. Over the years, these structural differences in schools have been either undetected or disregarded. Instead, reforms have been directed more often at those matters where effective and ineffective schools do not differ, such as basic modes of instruction, the nature of classroom activities, and the mechanics of teaching. Michael Sedlack and colleagues (1986) apparently agree with this appraisal of the situation.

> Not one of these [reform] proposals, however, takes into account the most fundamental variables in the educational process: the nature of the relationship between educators and their students and the extent to which students are actively engaged in the learning process. (p. ix)

THE ADOLESCENT SUBCULTURE

As early as the 1920s and 1930s, the Lynds (1929) found that high school students in Middletown had little interest in academic work; only a few students saw academics as the primary or even the secondary reason for attending school. Hollingshead (1949) found the same pattern of student disengagement from learning in his 1941 study of *Elmtown's Youth*. These early community studies provided the first empirical evidence of the adolescent subculture operating in the schools. Coupled with our theoretical understanding of the economic impetus underlying the

growth of schooling, such studies support the notion that the development of this subculture paralleled the expansion of schools.

Following these early reports, there have been many excellent quan-
titative studies further documenting the existence and effects of the
adolescent subculture that is anchored in the schools. Remmers and
Radler (1957) asked American teenagers to identify "the most important
thing young people should get out of high school." Only 14 percent of
the respondents listed "academics" as their answer. Almost thirty years
later, John Goodlad (1984) asked his sample of high school students,
"What is the one best thing about this school?" The responses were as
follows (adapted from Goodlad, 1984, pp. 76–77):

Response	Percentage
My friends	35
Sports	13
Good student attitudes	11
Nothing	8
Classes I'm taking	7
Teachers	4
Other	22

These findings dramatize the inconsequential place of academic learning in the lives of students.

If students had more to say about it, there would be even less
academic emphasis than currently exists. Goodlad (1984, p. 64) asked
parents, teachers, and students to cite the one goal that the schools
seemed to emphasize most. The choices were intellectual, social, personal, and vocational goals. He also asked members of each group to
identify which goal they would *prefer* to see emphasized. Among high
school students, 62 percent said that intellectual goals were most emphasized, but only 27 percent would prefer this state of affairs. Of
course, it would be naive to envision students wanting more rather than
less academic work. The real problem is whether student preferences
interfere with academic work.

The classic and probative study was conducted by James Coleman
(1961) and published as *The Adolescent Society*. Not only did Coleman
confirm the salience of an adolescent subculture in the schools; more
important, he convincingly demonstrated the relationship between a
strong youth culture and poor academic outcomes. Coleman asked students to identify whose disapproval (of a school activity) would be most
difficult to accept—parents', teachers', or friends'. Only 3 percent were
concerned with their teachers' disapproval; 54 percent and 43 percent,

respectively, were concerned about their parents' and friends' rejection. Coleman asked the students how they would best like to be remembered. Overwhelmingly, boys wanted to be remembered as an athletic star, and girls as either the most popular or an activities leader. Neither sex indicated any interest in being remembered as a brilliant student. Coleman also asked the students to speculate about their parents' preferences for their success in school. Their responses were patently supportive of the values of the adolescent subculture, leading Coleman (1961) to conclude that "even the rewards a child gains from his parents may help reinforce the values of the adolescent culture" (p. 34).

Of course, the existence of an adolescent subculture does not necessarily mean the demise of academic learning. Or does it? For each of the 10 schools in his sample, Coleman computed a school "value climate" reflecting the relative importance of academics, sports, and social activities to students in the school. Although nonacademic values were dominant in all schools (as noted above), Coleman ranked each school in terms of its relative emphasis on the adolescent value system. This made it possible to examine the influence of the adolescent subculture on academic achievements. (This is essentially the procedure that I used in Chapter 5.) Coleman found that the adolescent climate was negatively related to educational aspirations and homework, even though each of these depends to a greater degree on family background and on the amount of homework assigned by teachers.

Comparing schools where the adolescent value climate was weakest (that is, where more people valued good grades and brilliant students) with those where it was strongest, Coleman found that the IQ scores of students with good grades were higher in the former situation. Coleman (1961, p. 260) accounts for this somewhat perplexing finding by noting that "highly rewarded" activities breed widespread competition, which makes the most able participants likely to become the strongest achievers. When activities like academic learning go relatively unrewarded, however, the most able may be less motivated to compete, thus allowing their less able counterparts to exhibit the highest levels of achievement. Thus, Coleman (1961, p. 265) concludes that the presence of a strong adolescent value system in school "exerts a rather strong deterrent to academic achievement."

During the 1960s and 1970s numerous researchers generated considerable support for Coleman's findings about the negative academic effects of the adolescent subculture. McDill and Rigsby (1973), for instance, compared the effects of various aspects of an adolescent value climate on student achievement relative to other characteristics, including home socioeconomic background, individual scholastic ability, individual values, and school-level socioeconomic context. They found a clear relationship between the adolescent climate variables and math achievement, even after the other variables had been controlled simultaneously. Moreover, these researchers found that the adolescent climate was the only school-level variable accounting for some variation in achievement. Individual ability explained the greatest amount of achievement variation, followed by home socioeconomic status, personal values, and then the adolescent subculture. A number of formal school characteristics were shown to be unrelated to student academic outcomes. The work of McDill and associates (1967) was, in turn, extended and further supported by the studies of Brookover and colleagues (1979, 1982), Campbell and Alexander (1965), Clasen and Brown (1986), Cusik (1973, 1983), Goodlad (1984), Kandel and Lesser (1969), Larkin (1979), and Willis (1977). The conclusion is inescapable, and McDill and associates stated it succinctly in 1967: "In those schools where academic competition, intellectualism and subject matter competence are emphasized and rewarded by faculty and student bodies, individual students tend to conform to the scholastic norms of the majority and achieve at a higher level" (p. 199).

More recently, Goodlad (1984) concluded that "junior and senior high school youth are excessively preoccupied with physical appearance, popularity in the peer group, and games and athletics" (p. 75). He notes that there is nothing new in these findings except perhaps "the apparent intensity of these nonacademic interests. . . . [and] why we have taken so little practical account of them in school" (p. 75). He further captures my sentiments when he declares (p. 76) that a "potential for explosion exists . . . in the present disjuncture between elements of the youth culture on the one hand and the orientation of teachers and conduct of school on the other."

Goodlad (1984) makes the point that the influence of peer groups on individuals is growing as the influence of the family decreases. In our society, large increases in employed mothers and fathers, coupled with increasing divorce and single-parent households, create a family ill-equipped to supplement the work of the school. This contemporary family has seen its former influence on children shift to the peer group. In a study of the daily lives of children, Boocock (1976) found that children spend most of their time outside school with friends or alone, working or watching television, or "fooling around." Powell and Powell (1983) fear that the adolescent subculture is increasingly what school is all about, implying that schools might cease to exist if adolescent values and goals were somehow constrained. Such conclusions broadly resonate with Coleman's (1961) warning that coeducation "may be inimical to *both* academic achievement *and* social adjustment" (p. 51).

EGALITARIANISM AND ADOLESCENCE

During the past century our society has successfully moved toward universal, egalitarian schooling. In some respects, this achievement has exacerbated the problems associated with the adolescent subculture.

> At the turn of the century, [public schools] shared with private schools in the education of a small, elite student population preparing, for the most part, for higher education. Today, it educates an extraordinarily diverse student body from families varying widely in their expectations for education. Many of the boys and girls graduating from elementary schools and moving up into junior and senior high schools are not clients in any sense of the word. They go to school until the age of 16 or more because society requires it—and, of course, their friends are there. (Goodlad, 1984, p. 9)

In America, public schools are comprehensive, relatively nonselective, relatively egalitarian, and highly inclusive institutions. They accept the gifted and the handicapped, the affluent and the poor, those who are motivated and those who are simply required to attend. This great political achievement of the country amounts to nearly equal educational opportunity. Accordingly, efforts at educational reform require utmost protection of the progress our society has made toward becoming more just.

Some critics of school reform (McDill, Natriello, & Pallas, 1985) have reservations about its "failure to give balanced emphasis to the ideas of quality and equality" (p. 416) (see also Astin, 1982; Coleman, 1981; Finn, 1983; Gardner, 1961; Linn, Madaus, & Pedulla, 1982; Sedlak et al., 1986; Stedman & Smith, 1983). Long before equal educational opportunity was a near reality, John Gardner (1961) anticipated these reservations by asking, "*Can We Be Equal and Excellent Too?*" Reform measures, such as more rigorous and restricted curricula, greater demands for student time in school and on homework, and minimum competency testing, the critics argue, may spawn greater student stratification and failure. Critics fear that the negative effects of such reforms would fall disproportionately on those most in need of help from the schools. Indeed, the concern is that some reforms might be inegalitarian and elitist.

Women and racial minorities, in particular, have gained equal educational opportunities through the public schools, particularly mixed-sex schools. Historically, as discussed in Chapters 1 and 2, women were first excluded entirely from schools and then admitted and allowed to attend only segregated schools. Integrated and mixed-sex schools have only recently become fashionable and required by law. Thus, approximately equal educational achievement is a recent reality for women. It is understandable, therefore, that any educational reform that carries the risk of a reduced commitment to equality, in the name of quality, will be viewed with suspicion. And this is as it should be.

Nonetheless, our commitments to equality and universality constrain the public schools to housing an increasingly powerful adolescent subculture. "Student inclusiveness is the reality most high schools must cope with: the students are *different* and they are *there*. At the level of institutional policy, schools accommodate to this situation by providing something for everyone" (Powell et al., 1985, p. 2). The result, according to these authors, is "The Shopping Mall High School," an educational institution characterized by accommodation and mediocrity.

Of course, private schools have been able to avoid this conflict of equality and quality. Generally, they have had the luxury of student selection, allowing them not only students of higher ability and higher socioeconomic status, but also a less volatile adolescent subculture. Public schools, however, must persist along the path of equality and universality; they must discover a way to either harness or diffuse the effects of the adolescent subculture.

The ramifications of the adolescent subculture for school reform and, more specifically, for single- and mixed-sex schooling are pervasive and complex. In 1961, Coleman offered this advice:

> If secondary education is to be successful, it must successfully compete with cars and sports and social activities for the adolescents' attention, in an open market. The adolescent is no longer a child, but will spend his energies in the ways he sees fit. It is up to the adult society to so structure secondary education that it captures this energy. (p. 329)

Our challenge is, therefore, to create an *academic subculture* sufficiently powerful to counteract the adolescent subculture, yet politically sensitive enough to allay the fears of those groups whose relatively equal educational opportunities have been hard won and recent.

CREATING AN ACADEMIC SUBCULTURE

At the heart of the duplicity of goals noted above is the conflict that exists between the goals of teachers and those of students—a conflict between the life of the mind and of the body, a life of reading, thinking, and intellectual sharing versus a life of playing sports, dancing, or just hanging out. I avoid presenting the students' interests as primarily sexual because I doubt the predominance of sexual motives. The adolescent value system is complex, genuine, healthy, physical, valuable, and suffused with practical rationality. In and of itself, it is functional and productive for adolescents in their overall sociohistorical situation. It is, however, dysfunctional with respect to the cognitive academic development of adolescents and the academic goals of the school. This value conflict is at the heart of the crisis of schooling. Any successful strategy for reforming schools must discover acceptable ways to deactivate or reduce the energy of the adolescent value system, or at least rechannel that energy into scholastic endeavors.

One strategy for doing this, according to Goodlad (1984), is to reduce the size of our schools (not class size). His study of 38 schools showed that the most effective schools were relatively small. He notes that other studies support this conclusion across a variety of academic outcome areas. According to Goodlad (1984, p. 370) "it appears to be more difficult in small schools for the more extreme peer group values to take hold" (see also Barker & Gump, 1964).

Another strategy from Goodlad (1984) is an earlier beginning and ending to school. He proposes that school begin at age 4 and end at age 16. This recommendation would also help reduce the conflict between educational and adolescent values, since that conflict peaks between the ages of 12 and 18, especially the latter of these years. The idea would entail no additional costs; in fact, it would assist parents economically by saving the costs of day care for four-year-old children.

Coleman's (1961) solution was to channel the energies and values of youth toward the idea of academic competition. He found that academics, unlike sports, were an unrewarded activity, and hence they were pursued passively and reluctantly. He recommended offering more realistic rewards and prizes for academic achievement both within and between schools. With considerable foresight, he seems to have anticipated the "choice" movement, whereby parents and students would be allowed to choose which public school to attend rather than being assigned to the neighborhood school. If appropriate rewards were tied to academic success, the best students would be attracted to this type of activity. And if a particular school or group of schools were to consistently outperform other schools, more of the better students would be attracted to the schools where the academic subculture had become dominant. Unfortunately, this idea entails the possibility of creating a school system with an increasing degree of inequality.

Another approach is to separate potentially troublesome students from other students in the schools. Although this practice may seem undemocratic and/or inegalitarian, Hamilton (1986) notes that it is actually one of four important characteristics of successful dropout-prevention programs. Hamilton states that John Rawls' (1971) *Theory of Justice* helps to clarify a policy of separatism. Considering how inequalities might be justified in a democratic society, Rawls proposed that they could be considered "just" only if the inequality benefited those at the lowest level. In a similar manner, Feldblum, Krent and Watkin (1986) argue that the legal doctrine of "compensatory purpose" can be employed to justify the continued existence of separate female organizations. Historically, this argument has proven ineffective as an educational policy. Ability grouping, for example, is now generally viewed as more costly to those in the lowest group in terms of both achievement and self-image (Oakes, 1985; Rosenbaum, 1980). In the case of potential dropouts, however, Hamilton believes that differential treatment can sometimes be justified. Among the necessary conditions for this are that the "probable consequences of assignment to the lowest group be favorable and acceptable to those students and their parents" (Hamilton, 1986, p. 158).

In their study of public and private schools, Coleman, Hoffer, and Kilgore (1982) report that Catholic schools provide a more effective learning environment and better academic outcomes than public schools. They concluded (1982) that "the constraints imposed on schools in the public sector seem to impair their functioning as educational institutions, without providing the more egalitarian outcomes that are one of the goals of public schooling" (p. 185). Those authors strongly imply that the effectiveness of Catholic schools is due in large part to school policy, value consensus, and the authority of the schools to impose a greater degree of order and discipline. The implication is that school officials can cultivate an academic subculture if they are free from certain external constraints and are able to draw on a supportive parental community.

In a critical analysis of Coleman and associates' (1982) *High School Achievement,* however, McPartland and McDill (1982) fault them "for failing to consider the social context of the student body as a source of different learning environments" (p. 79). McPartland and McDill argue that the relatively low performance of students in public high schools may result mainly from the increased number of students from lower socioeconomic backgrounds who are concentrated in separate schools. McPartland and McDill propose that student body composition (particularly racial and socioeconomic) varies across schools and school types and that such variation accounts for differences in school climates,

which subsequently influence cognitive outcomes and school effectiveness in general.

McPartland and McDill's (1982) point is that the racial and socioeconomic composition of public schools is not a school policy variable.
It takes shape from the demography of neighborhoods and communities, along with prevailing local, state, and federal laws regarding racial
integration. Thus, the outcomes of schooling have a lot to do with the
demographic concentrations of students that create recalcitrant adolescent value climates in schools. In contrast to Coleman and associates,
McPartland and McDill urge school policy makers to reconsider the
current allocation practices that determine student body enrollments in
our nation's schools.

SINGLE–SEX SCHOOLING

Another possibility for reducing the influence of the adolescent subculture is some form of single-sex schooling—at least as an alternative, at
least at the classroom level, at least temporarily. As Chapters 3, 4, and 5
demonstrate, the adolescent subculture is diminished in all-girls schools,
and the academic performance of girls in these schools exceeds that of
their female counterparts in mixed-sex schools. All-girls schools exhibit a
low level of typical adolescent values and a *high* degree of order and/or
discipline. I speculate that the order follows as a matter of course from
the low adolescent orientation in these schools.

In all-boys schools, on the other hand, we discovered a *high* adolescent subculture together with a *high* level of discipline. I speculate here
that the discipline is imposed from without—the adolescent value system calls forth a high level of discipline in the schools. As noted in
Chapter 5, these somewhat puzzling results reveal an interesting process—namely, that in male single-sex schools, the adolescent context is
positively related to achievement. A high adolescent value system brings
about a high level of discipline, which in turn facilitates a high level of
learning. This differs from female single-sex schools, where the adolescent context is negatively related to both discipline and achievement.

In a rather surprising way, the high adolescent value climate found
in all-boys schools is actually conducive to greater academic achievement. I do not wish to argue that this process is desirable, ideal, or even
effective. Rather, I advocate the model manifested in all-girls schools.
Academically, these schools provide the basis for a truly effective education. Providing order in schools as a reaction to disorder is obviously
inefficient, even though the process does offer an educational advan-

tage to boys in single-sex schools. I would hasten to add that in the regular Catholic school sample, males in mixed-sex schools did better than males in single-sex schools, despite a whole set of background and school advantages favoring the latter. Of course, other processes are also at work in the schools, and we should take account of some of them by reviewing the overall results at this time.

As Chapter 5 demonstrates, the short-term cognitive effects of single-sex schooling differ according to race and sex. Minority females profit most from single-sex schooling, followed by minority males, and then by white females in the regular Catholic school sample. I estimate that white males in single-sex schools in the regular sample score lower than their peers in mixed-sex schools, after controlling for initial ability and home background. These results derive from the average-adjusted, senior-year test score differences for the four curriculum-specific tests shown in Table 5.7. This short-term cognitive effect among white females and no effect for white males is confirmed in a totally different study analyzed in Chapter 6 (see Table 6.7).

In Chapter 6, the positive effects of single-sex schools were shown to have substantial long-term results. Women who attended single-sex colleges have higher educational and occupational achievement, higher self-esteem and self-control, greater marital happiness, and more supportive views of equal sex roles than women who attended mixed-sex colleges. Likewise, women who graduated from single-sex high schools were found to have higher cognitive ability (seven years beyond high school) than women who graduated from mixed-sex schools. Among white males, the long-term cognitive effects parallel the outcomes in Chapter 5, confirming that male students in mixed-sex schools attain equal or higher cognitive achievement than those in single-sex schools. Insufficient data were available to analyze the long-term outcomes among male minority students. With regard to educational and occupational attainment, males graduating from single-sex schools do better than those from mixed-sex schools. This latter result is due almost entirely to the considerable home socioeconomic advantage enjoyed by students who attend male single-sex Catholic schools.

What is to be made of these short- and long-term results? Apparently, the findings confirm that the effects of school are greater among students from disadvantaged homes. Coleman and associates (1966, p. 299) reported this in *Equality of Educational Opportunity*. More recently, using these same HSB data, Hoffer, Greeley, and Coleman (1985) have shown that the effects of Catholic schools vis-à-vis public schools are greater for black, Hispanic, and lower socioeconomic status students. The explanatory logic is both appealing and simple. Home background is a potent influence on school achievement as long as the home is minimally advantaged, that is, working- or middle-class. If the home is disadvantaged, however, by virtue of low socioeconomic or minority group status, then the potential effects of the home are small and probably even negative. When the potential influence of the home on learning is minimal or negative, the potential effects of the school increase. When the influence of the home is large, schools have only minimal influence. This same pattern holds for the influence of gender context.

The effects of single-sex schools are greatest among Hispanic and black female students in the minority sample. Generally, these students are disadvantaged by their home background and their female status. They have, in effect, three low-status characteristics: female, low socioeconomic status, and racial/ethnic minority status. Hispanic and black males in the minority sample have two low-status characteristics: low socioeconomic status and racial/ethnic minority status. Similarly, white females in the regular sample have a single low-status characteristic—female.

In the regular school sample, white males in single-sex schools have no negative ascribed-status characteristics. Why then, do their male counterparts in mixed-sex schools predict higher test scores on average? Conceivably, as Shaw (1980, p. 71) has argued, males in mixed-sex schools may obtain an advantage by comparing themselves as a group to females, who may serve as a negative reference group. This inclination is especially likely in math and science, where girls score lower than boys. In predominantly white, all-male schools, on the other hand, no such negative reference group is available. Consequently, in the competitive environment of schools, some white males will become low performers. To the extent that this is true, the overall cognitive scores of boys in single-sex schools would decrease. In any event, similar findings have been reported by Dale (1971, 1974) and more recently by Lockheed and Komenan (1988).

The same forces operate in all-male schools in the minority sample and in all-female schools. Offsetting those forces, however, are other factors, including greater receptivity for school effects among low-status students and the effects of the adolescent subculture and role modeling (see below and Chapter 3). These results for both males and females in the regular sample seem to confirm that coeducational schools are really boys' schools; that is, they mainly serve the interests of boys (Ingalls, 1984; Shaw, 1980).

Aside from the advantages that accrue to boys in mixed-sex schools in the regular sample, females in single-sex schools in both samples outperform their female peers in mixed-sex schools. In the minority school sample, this single-sex advantage applies to boys as well. Considering the four curriculum-specific tests, the background-adjusted, single-sex school advantage among females and minority school males averages about 0.7 of a grade equivalent over a two-year period (see Table 5.7). Of this difference, two-thirds, on average, derives from the set of school variables—curriculum, course work, homework, and the adolescent subculture. Thus, the formal and informal structures of single-sex schools apparently offer mechanisms for increasing the educational achievement of students.

What would account for the remaining test score advantage of students in single-sex schools? A likely explanation lies in the theory of role modeling, discussed in Chapter 3. The argument applies especially to females, because all-girls schools are taught and administered predominantly by women. In these schools, successful female student role models exist in all subjects. In all-girls schools the heroines are neither athletes nor homecoming queens; the valedictorians and scholarship winners are girls, not boys. In mixed-sex schools, on the other hand, the role models are successful male athletes or scholars, homecoming queens and cheerleaders, and male as well as female staff.

To a lesser extent, the role modeling theory also applies to males in single-sex minority schools, where the percentage of academically successful males is greater than in mixed-sex schools. In fact, a greater percentage of the single-sex advantage is explained for males in the minority sample than for females in either sample. For males in the minority sample, the school factors explain 100 percent of the average test score difference, whereas the school variables explain only 38 percent of the advantage for females in the minority sample and only 40 percent for females in the regular sample. The greater unexplained difference among females suggests that the theory of role modeling is more applicable to them than to the boys in the minority sample. Of course, role modeling is also applicable to all-boys schools in the regular sample but is apparently offset by the aforementioned process whereby males in mixed-sex schools succeed at the expense of females.

In addition to the effects of role models in single-sex schools, Chapter 3 notes the possibility of less sex bias among teachers and peers in single-sex schools. Mixed-sex interaction consistently involves male dominance, and teachers may favor males in mixed-sex classrooms. Lastly, as we discovered in Chapter 4, the cost of tuition for girls attending single-sex schools presented a financial sacrifice. These girls come from homes of lower socioeconomic status than girls attending mixed-sex schools, and their schools operate almost entirely on the basis of tuition. This economic burden undoubtedly generates additional commitment to academic values. This may account for the high educational aspirations of girls in single-sex schools (see Table 4.3), and may, in turn, lead to higher academic performance. Consequently, single-sex schools are likely to be characterized by a set of values generally *shared* by parents, students, and teachers, which stress the importance of family and education. Hence, a choice of single-sex education is more of a pro-academic choice; whereas a choice of mixed-sex schooling may be a choice in favor of the adolescent subculture.

AN ALTERNATIVE FORM OF EDUCATIONAL REFORM

This book argues the case for reconsidering the merits of single-sex schooling. The question of single- versus mixed-sex schooling is complex. There are pros and cons on either side. Yet sufficient grounds now exist for reconsidering the potential of single-sex schooling, at least as an option representing an alternative to mixed-sex schools. It merits exploration on an experimental and limited basis. Single-sex education could be housed within existing mixed-sex schools and limited to the classroom only. Whatever form it might take, it should be offered as an alternative, in the same way as magnet schools, open space classrooms, team taught classrooms, and school voucher plans.

There is at least as much empirical support in favor of single-sex schools (or classes) for girls as there is for magnet schools, smaller schools, or a longer school year. A policy of single-sex schooling requires virtually no new or additional teachers, buildings, or training. In addition, it is more effective (in terms of academic outcomes), more economical (in terms of the number of teachers and administrative staff required), and easier to implement than all of the following commonly mentioned proposals for educational reform:

1. Reducing class size
2. Lengthening the school day or year
3. Preschool and after-school help for children at risk
4. Greater parental involvement
5. Upgrading educational training for teachers and/or principals
6. Reorganizing the teaching profession
7. Upgrading and standardizing school curricula
8. Minimum competency testing
9. More demanding high school graduation requirements
10. Magnet schools

Many of the above reforms represent attempts to increase the amount of instructional exposure available to students. The notions of "engaged time" or "active-learning" time are the buzz words among reformers of the 1980s. The relationship of time-on-task to academic achievement is generally accepted as gospel among educational reformers and classroom teachers. Engaged learning time can be increased by simply decreasing the impact of the adolescent subculture. Of course, it can also be increased, albeit in costly ways, by lengthening the school day or the school year. Not only are the latter reforms more expensive, but they are likely to be inefficient, because they fail to contain the countervailing influences of a nonacademic value system.

Historically, mixed-sex schools were, of course, more economically efficient. As pointed out in Chapters 1 and 2, the vast majority of schools worldwide became mixed-sex schools on the basis of economic, rather than pedagogic, principles. In the past most countries' sparsely settled land made it economically difficult to establish separate schools for boys and girls. In most large urban areas today, this circumstance no longer applies. Although many single-sex colleges and high schools have closed or gone coeducational for economic reasons, this has not been due to population sparsity. Instead, it is a direct result of the impact of the adolescent subculture. Adolescent values, not educational values, have led to the demise of single-sex schooling. Economic factors today allow for reversing that trend; they allow educational values to supersede extracurricular values in contemporary schools.

The support for single-sex schooling does not rest solely on academic outcomes, nor does it depend entirely on the results of the empirical analyses reported in Chapters 5 and 6. Chapter 3 reviewed a full range of theoretical views and other empirical studies that, taken as whole, consistently point to the efficacy of single-sex education, especially for women.

In summary, single-sex schools offer an environment that is more conducive to learning than mixed-sex schools, especially for women. They provide more role models for students, and they offer more order and control than mixed-sex schools. In all-girls schools, the adolescent climate is weak, allowing an academic climate to flourish. In all-boys schools, the adolescent climate is strong, but it is accompanied by a strong disciplinary structure. For women and minority males, these schools produce favorable academic outcomes over both the short and long term in terms of cognitive ability, and educational and occupational attainment.

Both males and females in mixed-sex schools are likely to experience some sex bias from teachers, counselors, or fellow students. Sex bias in single-sex schools is minimal. Single-sex schools may promote more traditional sex-role development, while mixed-sex schools are commonly assumed to offer greater opportunities for less traditional and more egalitarian sex-role learning. In practice, however, mixed-sex schools are typically sex segregated. Boys and girls still seem to prefer same-sex friends, and cross-sex interaction remains male-dominated.

Mixed-sex schools do provide equality of educational opportunity, de jure. Unfortunately, the law is limited and difficult to monitor. Beyond questions of admission, single-sex schools obviously do not discriminate by sex in providing educational opportunity. Finally, contrary to the coeducational argument, the affective or personal growth outcomes also favor single-sex schools, especially with regard to women. No negative attitudinal or affective outcomes accrue to women who attend single-sex schools.

Single-sex education has received little attention, partly due to a fear that it may undercut women's long-sought and hard-won gains for equality of education. Some people see the idea as inescapably reactionary and unacceptable. Single-sex (segregated) education does conjure up images of various elitist and invidious educational practices, including selective and denominational schooling and proposals for tuition tax credits. Some feminists may see any form of "separatism" as negatively affecting women's equal access in other areas of society. Thus, discussions of single-sex and mixed-sex schooling must address such misgivings. One way to alleviate some of these reservations is to lay bare the typical reality of most mixed-sex classrooms and schools, notwithstanding the improvements wrought by Title IX. This may ease the concerns of those who fear that single-sex schooling is anachronistic in an egalitarian age.

Another way to alleviate misgivings is to emphasize that single-sex education need not be equated with single-sex schools. In *The Shopping Mall High School*, Powell and colleagues (1985) declare that the schools have accommodated to diversity by providing something for everybody; that is, by providing more variety. Within the context of specialty shops, course variety, and choice, is it not possible and meaningful to explore *voluntary* grouping by sex? Is it not desirable for schools to offer single-sex classes in some subjects for those who might choose this option? Is it not promising to explore single-sex public schools on some limited, experimental basis? Is it not important to urge a halt to further closing of existing single-sex colleges and high schools? Does it not make sense to learn more about the potential efficacy of single-sex educational environments before they become historical artifacts?

Despite evidence demonstrating that single-sex schools are no more or less divisive than mixed-sex schools, the fear of divisiveness persists. The plain fact of the matter is that the "common school" myth pervades American education. With the single exception of resistance to racial integration, the ideal of educating everyone alike has led to a misperception of public and coeducational schools as egalitarian, and private or single-sex schooling as inegalitarian. That same misperception has bred unrealistic fears of new options in both public and private schooling. In view of the crisis of education today, we need to explore and promote creative alternatives to our current forms of public and private schooling. This effort requires that we remain steadfast in our commitments to equality and universality, while renewing the educational quality of our schools. Accomplishing this means that an academic culture must become fashionable in the schools. It means protecting and preserving existing single-sex schools in the private sector. In the public schools, it means providing some limited and exploratory single-sex schools or classrooms as alternatives to mixed-sex schools for students who want a first-rate education or who might be encouraged or persuaded to undertake one.

BEYOND AMERICA

In many nations across the world, single-sex schooling is the norm for many students, or at least the type of schooling attended by a substantial minority. Table 1.2 of Chapter 1 summarizes the extent of single-sex schooling in 19 countries that participated in the first International Study of Education. Although these data are from the 1960s and thus may be dated, 11 of the 20 countries provide single-sex schools to at least 32 percent of the student population at the compulsory level. Absent from this list of countries, but offering predominantly single-sex schooling, are Ireland and Jamaica, as well as many Middle Eastern and African countries. Single-sex education is well established in some countries, despite the overall world trend toward coeducation.

The dictates of an increasingly technological economy are recognized to affect the nature of educational systems around the globe. In developing countries, the shift to white-collar, technical, professional, and managerial occupations has led to the need for more efficient, effective, and widespread education. Education becomes increasingly important in occupational recruitment and training as nations become more technological and industrial. The result is an increasing dependence on an effective educational system.

In developing or underdeveloped countries, in particular, an effective educational system is critical. One might argue that the system should be even more effective than in developed countries, in view of the technological, industrial, and economic gaps that exist. Fortunately, some data show that "school effects" are greater in developing countries than in developed countries. Despite fairly consistent evidence from studies in the United States showing that school characteristics are not strongly related to student achievement (Fuller, 1986; Hanushek, 1986), studies of student achievement in developing countries have found otherwise. Heyneman and Loxley (1983) report that in developing countries the effects of school quality are substantial in comparison with home and other background factors (see also Heyneman & Jamison, 1980; Jamison & Lockheed, 1987; Psacharopoulos & Arriagada, 1987; Simmons & Alexander, 1978). These reports parallel American studies (cited above) demonstrating greater school effects among students from disadvantaged homes.

In fact, studies are beginning to emerge specifically confirming the effectiveness of single-sex education for women in developing countries. Lockheed and Komenan (1988) report a study of school effects on student achievement in Nigeria and Swaziland. Students attending all-female schools "performed significantly better than students in coeducational schools. In Swaziland, boys in all-male schools perform significantly less well than students in coeducational schools" (pp. 28–29). In the Nigerian schools, there were no significant differences in achievement between boys in single- and mixed-sex schools. These results parallel those reported in Chapters 5 and 6. Other studies showing positive results for girls in single-sex schools can be found in Thailand (Jimenez & Lockheed, 1989; Klainin & Fesham, 1986), in Nigeria (Lee & Lockheed, 1989) and in Jamaica (Hamilton, 1985).

Aside from the special problems of developing countries, we must note that educational achievement in the United States stands considerably below that of comparable industrialized and westernized countries. Indeed, this circumstance has alarmed the various commissions reporting on the state of American education. In the first project of the International Association for the Evaluation of Educational Achievement (IEA), conducted during the 1960s, the United States scored significantly below Japan, Belgium, Australia, Israel, England, and the Netherlands on a standardized mathematics test (Husen, 1967). Twenty years later, this situation persists. In the second International Mathematics Study, conducted during the 1980s, the United States scored only average among 24 other countries (Ballantine, 1989). Of perhaps even greater importance, Hanna and Kuendiger (1986) found that on this second

IEA mathematics test, girls were more successful in relation to boys in several countries, including Belgium, Thailand, Finland, and Hungary. The United States was among several countries where boys were more successful than girls. For most of the countries considered, there were no significant differences between the sexes on the mathematics test. On the science section of this second IEA study, Postlethwaite (1988) reports that the United States scored far below average in comparison with 17 other countries.

The educational system of each country is deeply embedded in a historical and cultural past. Many countries still provide an educational system that is predominantly single-sex. In others, single-sex classes are available in coeducational schools. Some of these single-sex educational systems are remarkably effective. In any event, the United States is in no position to hold out its educational system as a model. Bearing this in mind, we need to intensify our understanding of other national educational systems. At the same time, as I hope I have shown, we need to implement exploratory and experimental programs of our own. In my judgment as a social scientist and educational researcher, the most promising of these programs give students some measure of access to single-sex education.

APPENDIX

Controlling for Home Background and Initial Ability

To control for the effects of initial ability and home background, the data analyses in Chapters 5 and 6 use a statistical technique called regression standardization. This allows us to *estimate* the effects of single- and mixed-sex schools under an *as if* scenario. That is, what would be the difference between the two school types, if the students who attended them were otherwise equal in ability and home background? Of course, it is seldom possible to control for all relevant background characteristics. The possibility always remains that differences that may be attributed to school type are instead due to some unmeasured aspect of the student's background, ability, or motivation. Consider the following example based on actual data from the science test.

Boys in single-sex schools obtained a score of 12.5 on the senior science test. To determine the relative impact of key predictor variables on this score, I will regress the senior science score for boys in single-sex schools on these predictor variables. For the sake of simplicity I will use only the pre-test and the socioeconomic composite as predictor variables in this example. The resulting statistical analysis produces the following equation:

$$Y = a + [(b_1) \times (X_1)] + [(b_2) \times (X_2)]$$

post-test science score	=	constant	+	pre-test effect	×	pre-test mean	+	SES effect	×	SES mean
	=	5.57	+	[0.6	×	11.1]	+	[0.7	×	0.45]
	=	5.57	+	6.66			+	0.315		
	=	12.5								

157

Note that b represents the effect of a variable and is multiplied by the mean or variable average. The overall effect of socioeconomic status is very small relative to that of the pre-test.

The regression equation allows for a what-if-everybody-were-the-same analysis. Substituting the mean scores of male students in mixed-sex schools in the equation allows us to predict the scores that males in single-sex schools would achieve if their initial abilities and home backgrounds were the same as those of students in mixed-sex schools. Thus:

predicted post-test score if males in single-sex schools had the background characteristics of males in mixed-sex schools	= constant	+	pre-test effect	×	pre-test mean of males in mixed-sex schools	+ SES effect	×	SES mean of males in mixed-sex schools
	=	5.57	+ [0.6	×	10.8]	+ [0.7	×	0.37]
	=	12.3						

The raw senior test score difference between male students in single- and mixed-sex schools is reduced by controlling or adjusting for initial ability and home background. The raw uncontrolled difference between males in single- and mixed-sex schools is 0.6 (12.5 − 11.9), while the adjusted difference is 0.4 (12.3 − 11.9). This can be converted to a grade equivalent score of 0.7 by dividing by 0.6 (the average one-year gain on this test). Although these adjusted scores are only estimates, they clearly lie in the predicted direction. The science score of males in single-sex schools should decrease if their initial ability and socioeconomic status were lower (more like those of males in mixed-sex schools). This is, in fact, what happens.

The scores may also be adjusted by using the regression equation for males in mixed-sex schools. The equation may not be exactly the same because it is based on a different pattern of data (the data for males in mixed-sex schools). However, it should be fairly similar and it is.

post-test score = 5.76 + [0.54×pre-test mean] + [0.7×SES mean]

As an exercise, the reader is encouraged to compute the adjusted test score differences using this second equation. The equation is based upon males in mixed-sex schools, so the mean scores for males in single-sex schools will have to be inserted to make the standardization work. The resulting adjusted post-test score for males in mixed-sex schools (computed using the mean values from the single-sex sample) should be compared with the actual post-test mean of males in single-sex schools. The results turn out to be the same, 0.7 of a grade equivalent.

This procedure has the advantage of being relatively easy to understand. It has the disadvantage of providing two predicted and adjusted scores, as noted above. As long as the regression equations are not significantly different, it is preferable and easier to compute a single regression equation. (This is possible because the slopes of the two equations are, in fact, very similar.) The computation merges all the data in the above example and includes school type as one of the predictor variables in what is known as a general multiple regression equation. In this procedure, the overall effect of each predictor variable is computed under the statistical assumption that all students have the same levels of ability and home background. Thus, a standardization process is built into the statistical calculations that, in essence, equates respondents on every other variable. The resulting general regression equation then allows predictions about groups with certain average scores on specific variables. For the above example, the regression equation is:

predicted   = 5.57 + [0.4×school] + [0.56×pre-test] + [0.7×SES]
post-test   type   score   score
score

This procedure lets us simply assume that the pre-test and the socioeconomic level are the same (as noted above). Therefore, since school type will be coded 1 for single-sex and 0 for mixed-sex, the effect of school type *is* the adjusted raw post-test score. This score is then converted to a grade equivalent score: 0.4 / 0.6=0.7. This is, in fact, the adjusted science test score difference for males found in the previous examples. This adjusted diference is greater than the one shown in Table 5.2, because not all the elements of home background are in this equation.

The question arises as to how many of the pre-tests should be used in adjusting for initial ability. Nearly everyone who has worked with the data agrees that the specific pre-test must be included. Willms (1985) argues, however, that all three general achievement pre-tests should be used as controls for initial ability. Jencks (1985) concurs with Willms. Others (Alexander & Pallas, 1985; Hoffer et al., 1985; Lee & Bryk, 1986)

have chosen to use a single pre-test. Including all the general achievement tests virtually ensures that initial ability is fully controlled. Yet
this strategy carries the risk of overadjustment, which may conceal
the effects of school type. Using only the specific pre-test as a control
may, however, entail an underadjustment for initial ability. I analyzed
the data using both strategies and, after reviewing the results, opted to
use only the specific pre-test (see Riordan, 1987 for a detailed explanation).

Notes

CHAPTER 1

[1]In the Republic of Ireland (not shown in Table 1.2) nearly two-thirds of secondary schools are single-sex (see Hannon et al., 1983).

CHAPTER 3

[1]The 1954 Supreme Court decision in *Brown* v. *Board of Education,* which ordered the desegregation of American schools, was decided primarily on the constitutional principle of equal protection (Read, 1975). The academic and social benefits of desegregation, however, have always occupied an important role, both before and after the decision.

[2]There are, of course, other dependent variables (outcomes) associated with contact through desegregation, such as equalizing educational and occupational opportunity. For an extensive review of possible outcomes of racial desegregation, see Rossell and Hawley, 1983; St. John, 1975; and Stephan and Feagin, 1980.

[3]The original bill, proposed in 1970 by Congresswoman Edith Green (D., Ore.) would have had the effect of prohibiting single-sex schools entirely, but it never went further than the hearing stage. In early 1971, several alternative bills were proposed in the Senate and the House to prohibit sex discrimination in education. These proposals took varying stances ranging from full to partial provisions for the continued existence of single-sex schooling. For example, Representative Green's revised proposal of 1971 would have prohibited sex discrimination in all admissions policies with the exception of institutions that were all of one sex. Congressman Albert Qude (R., Minn.), however, was adamant that admissions policies should be exempt. In the Senate, similar political differences were manifested. The net result was a bill, passed by both the Senate and the House, that represented considerable compromise. With regard to admissions policies, Title IX ended up exempting elementary and secondary schools, military schools, religious schools, private undergraduate schools, and

public undergraduate schools that had continuously been single-sex schools. (For a complete and detailed review of the historical development of the Title IX legislation, see Fishel & Pottker, 1977a.)

⁴In British and European countries, the principle of equality of educational opportunity has been pursued in a somewhat parallel fashion under the general rubric of the "comprehensive school" movement (see Bellaby, 1977; Deem, 1978; Husen, 1974). Comprehensive schools, though they vary between countries, reflect in a representative way the social composition of the community outside the school. Unlike the situation in the United States, however, the movement toward comprehensive schools was intended, in great part, to eliminate sex and class discrimination thought to be caused by the continued existence of selective and elitist single-sex schools.

⁵Some data are available with regard to single-sex public vocational schools. These schools have been shown to provide a differential pattern of access to vocational training for boys and girls. The common practice is to provide girls and boys with programs that prepare them for traditionally sex-typed occupations (see Fishel & Pottker, 1977b).

⁶Clearly, modeling may become disadvantageous, as in Australia's schools of domestic science that provide students with "little alternative to the role of happy homemaking" (Bessant, 1976). Various proprietary schools in the United States may function in a similar manner. Such schools are beyond the scope of this book.

CHAPTER 6

¹I am grateful to the following organizations and individuals that provided information on women's colleges: The Women's College Coalition; Vance Grant, National Institute of Education; David Ray, National Institute of Independent Colleges and Universities. My list of schools ($N=136$) included two proprietary schools, several Jewish seminaries, and some colleges that had closed by 1976. Aside from the two proprietary schools, all of the schools offered at a minimum an Associate of Arts (AA) degree. Students from the proprietary schools were removed from further analysis in this study.

²Race is not related to college type. Minorities are as likely as whites to be in either type of school. Consequently race cannot operate as a common cause variable in this case. Moreover, the influence of race on both educational and occupational achievement is insignificant when socioeconomic status is controlled.

References

Alexander, Karl L. & Aaron M. Pallas. 1983. Private Schools and Public Policy: New Evidence on Cognitive Achievement in Public and Private Schools. *Sociology of Education* 56, 170–182.

Alexander, Karl L. & Aaron M. Pallas. 1984. In Defense of "Private Schools and Public Policy": A Reply to Kilgore. *Sociology of Education* 57, 56–58.

Alexander, Karl L. & Aaron M. Pallas. 1985. School Sector and Cognitive Performance: When is a Little a Little? *Sociology of Education* 58, 115–128.

Allport, Gordon W. 1958. *The Nature of Prejudice* (abr. ed.). Garden City, NJ: Doubleday.

Amir, Yehuda. 1976. The Role of Intergroup Contact in Change of Prejudice and Ethnic Relations. In Phyllis A. Katz (ed.), *Towards the Elimination of Racism*. New York: Pergamon Press, 245–308.

Appel, David & Eugene Freeman. 1962. *The Wisdom and Ideas of Plato*. New York: Fawcett World Library.

Arnot, Madeleine. 1983. A Cloud Over Coeducation: An Analysis of the Forms of Transmission of Class and Gender. In S. Walker & Z. Barton (eds.), *Gender, Class and Education*. London: Falmer Press, 69–91.

Ascik, Thomas R. 1984. An Investigation of School Desegregation and Its Effects on Black Student Achievement. *American Education* 20, 15–19.

Astin, Alexander S. 1982. Excellence and Equity in American Education. Paper prepared for the National Commission on Excellence in Education, Higher Education Research Institute, Inc., University of California, Los Angeles.

Astin, Alexander W. 1968. *The College Environment*. Washington, DC: American Council of Education.

Astin, Alexander W. 1977. *Four Critical Years*. San Francisco: Jossey-Bass.

Astin, Alexander W. & Robert J. Panos. 1969. *The Educational and Vocational Development of College Students*. Washington, DC: American Council of Education.

Astin, Helen & Werner Z. Hirsch. 1978. *The Higher Education Women: Essays in Honor of Rosemary Park*. New York: Praeger.

Atherton, B. F. 1972. Co-Educational and Single Sex Schooling and Happiness of Marriage. *Educational Research* 15, 221–226.

Austin, Joe D. 1979. Homework Research in Mathematics. *School Science and Math* 79, 115–121.

Ballantine, Jeanne H. 1989. *The Sociology of Education*. Englewood Cliffs, NJ: Prentice Hall.

Barker, Roger G. & Paul V. Gump. 1964. *Big School, Small School*. Stanford, CA: Stanford University Press.

Bauch, Patricia A. 1988. Differences Among Single-Sex and Co-educational High Schools. *Momentum* 19, 56–58.

Bellaby, Paul. 1977. *The Sociology of Comprehensive Schooling*. London: Methuen.

Benn, C. & B. Simon. 1972. *Half-way There*. Harmondsworth, NY: Penguin.

Bessant, Bob. 1976. Domestic Science Schools and Women's Place. *Australian Journal of Education* 20, 1–9.

Bingham, W. C. & E. W. House. 1977. Counselors' Attitudes Toward Women and Work. In Janice M. Pottker & Andrew Fishel (eds.), *Sex Bias in the Schools*. Teaneck, NJ: Fairleigh Dickenson University Press, 247–255.

Blackstone, Tessa. 1976. The Education of Girls Today. In Juliet Mitchell & Ann Oakley (eds.), *The Rights and Wrongs of Women*. Harmondsworth, NY: Penguin, 199–216.

Blau, Peter M. & Otis Dudley Duncan. 1967. *The American Occupational Structure*. New York: John Wiley.

Blum, John M. et al. 1984. *The National Experience*. San Diego: Harcourt Brace Jovanovich.

Boocock, Sarane S. 1976. *Students, Schools and Educational Policy: A Sociological View*. Cambridge, MA: Asper Institute for Humanistic Studies.

Boocock, Sarane S. 1980. *Sociology of Education: An Introduction* (2nd ed.). Boston: Houghton Mifflin.

Bowler, Sister Mary Marcella. 1933. *A History of Catholic Colleges for Women in the United States of America*. Washington, DC: The Catholic University of America.

Braddock, Jomills Henry, II, Robert L. Crain, & James M. McPartland. 1984. A Long-Term View of School Desegregation: Some Recent Studies of Graduates as Adults. *Phi Delta Kappan* 66, 259–264.

Brehony, Kevin, 1984. Co-education: Perspective and Debates in the Early Twentieth Century. In Rosemary Deem (ed.) *Co-Education Reconsidered*. Milton-Keynes, England: Open University Press, 1–20.

Brody, Linda & Lynn H. Fox. 1980. An Accelerative Intervention Program for Mathematically Gifted Girls. In Lynn H. Fox, Linda Brody, & Dianne Tobin (eds.), *Women and the Mathematical Mystique*. Baltimore: Johns Hopkins University Press, 164–178.

Brookover, Wilber et al. 1979. *School Social Systems and Student Achievement: Schools Can Make a Difference*. New York: Praeger.

Brookover, Wilber et al. 1982. *Creating Effective Schools*. Holmes Beach, FL: Learning Publications.

Brophy, Jere E. & Thomas L. Good. 1974. *Teacher–Student Relationship: Causes and Consequences*. New York: Holt, Rinehart & Winston.

Broverman, I. K., S. R. Vogel, D. M. Broverman, F. E. Clarkson, & P. Rosenkranz. 1972. Sex-Role Stereotypes: A Current Appraisal. *Journal of Social Issues* 28, 59–78.

Brown v. Board of Education. 1954. 347 U.S. 484.

Bruto, Michel. 1969. *The Necessarie, Fit and Convenient Education of a Young Gentlewoman.* New York: DeCapo Press. (Originally published in 1598.)

Bryk, Anthony S. 1981. Disciplined Inquiry or Policy Argument? *Harvard Educational Review* 51, 497–509.

Bryk, Anthony S., Peter B. Holland, Valerie E. Lee, & Ruben A. Carriedo. 1984. *Effective Catholic Schools: An Exploration.* Washington, DC: National Center for Research in Total Catholic Education.

Bureau of Education. 1883. *Co-education of the Sexes in the Public Schools of the U.S.A.* Washington, DC: United States Government Printing Office.

Burstyn, Joan N. 1980. *Victorian Education and the Ideal of Womanhood.* Totowa, NJ: Barnes & Noble.

Butler, Nicholas M. (ed.). 1910. *Education in the United States.* New York: American Book Company.

Byrne, Eileen, M. 1978. *Women and Education.* London: Tavistock Publications.

Campbell, Ernest Q. & N. Alexander. 1965. Structural Effects and Interpersonal Relations. *American Journal of Sociology* 71, 284–289.

Campbell, R. J. 1969. Co-education: Attitudes and Self-concepts of Girls at Three Schools. *British Journal of Educational Psychology* 39, 87.

Carithers, M. A. 1970. School Desegregation and Racial Cleavage 1957–1970: A Review of the Literature. *Journal of Social Issues* 26, 25–47.

Carnegie Commission on Higher Education. 1973. *Opportunities for Women in Higher Education.* New York: McGraw Hill.

Carpenter, Peter & Martin Hayden. 1987. Girls' Academic Achievement: Single-Sex Versus Coeducational Schools in Australia. *Sociology of Education* 60, 156–167.

Casserly, Patricia. 1978. Study Finds Girls are Diverted from Careers in Math and Science. *ETS Developments* 25(3), 4–5.

Clark, R. 1983. *Family Life and School Achievement: Why Poor Black Children Succeed and Fail.* Chicago: University of Chicago Press.

Clarke, Edward H. 1873. *Sex in Education: A Fair Chance for the Girls.* Boston: James R. Osgood and Company.

Clarke, Edward H. 1874. *The Building of a Brain.* Boston: James R. Osgood and Company.

Clasen, Donna & B. Bradford Brown. 1986. The Relationship Between Adolescent Peer Groups and School Performance. Paper presented at the annual meeting of the American Educational Research Association, San Francisco.

Cohen, Elizabeth G. & Susan S. Roper. 1972. Modification of Interracial Interaction Disability: An Application of Status Characteristic Theory. *American Sociological Review* 37, 643–657.

Cole, Robert Danforth. 1928. *Private Secondary Education for Boys in the United States.* Philadelphia: Westbrook Publishing Company.

Coleman, James S. 1961. *The Adolescent Society.* New York: The Free Press.

Coleman, James S. 1981. Quality and Inequality in American Education: Public and Private Schools. *Phi Delta Kappan* 63, 159–164.

Coleman, James S. 1987. Families and Schools. *Educational Researcher* 16, September–August, 32–38.

Coleman, James S., Ernest Q. Campbell, Carol J. Hobson, James McPartland, Alexander M. Mood, Frederic D. Weinfeld & Robert L. York. 1966. *Equality of Educational Opportunity.* Washington, DC: U.S. Government Printing Office.

Coleman, James S. & Thomas Hoffer. 1987. *Public and Private Schools: The Impact of Communities.* New York: Basic Books.

Coleman, James S., Thomas Hoffer, & Sally Kilgore. 1981. *Public and Private Schools* (Final Report). Washington, DC: National Center for Education Statistics.

Coleman, James, Thomas Hoffer, & Sally Kilgore. 1982. *High School Achievement: Public, Catholic and Private Schools Compared.* New York: Basic Books.

Comber, L. C. & J. P. Keeves. 1973. *Science Education in Nineteen Countries.* New York: Halsted Press.

Congressional Quarterly Almanac, 1971.

Conway, Jill K. 1974. Coeducation and Women's Studies: Two Approaches to the Question of Woman's Place in the Contemporary University. *Daedalus* 103, 239–249.

Cooper, Bruce S. 1988. The Changing Universe of U.S. Private Schools. In T. James & H. M. Levin (eds.), *Comparing Public and Private Schools.* Philadelphia: Falmer Press, 18–45.

Crain, Robert L., Rita E. Mahard, & Ruth E. Narot. 1982. *Making Desegregation Work: How Schools Create Social Climates.* Cambridge, MA: Ballinger Press.

Curwood, Steve. 1986. Black Colleges Draw New Interest. *Boston Sunday Globe*, May 18, 1, 24.

Cusik, Philip A. 1973. *Inside High School: The Student's World.* New York: Holt, Rinehart & Winston.

Cusik, Philip A. 1983. *The Egalitarian Ideal and the American High School.* New York: Longman.

Dale, Reginald R. 1971. *Mixed or Single-Sex Schools: Some Social Aspects, Vol. II.* London: Routledge & Kegan Paul.

Dale, Reginald R. 1974. *Mixed or Single-Sex Schools: Attainment, Attitudes, and Overview, Vol. III.* London: Routledge & Kegan Paul.

Deble, Isabelle. 1980. *The School Education of Girls.* Paris: United Nations Educational, Scientific, and Cultural Organization.

Deem, Rosemary. 1978. *Women and Schooling.* London: Routledge & Kegan Paul.

Deem, Rosemary (ed.). 1984. *Coeducation Reconsidered.* Milton Keynes, England: Open University Press.

Delamont, Sara. 1980. *Sex Roles and the School: Contemporary Sociology of the School.* London: Methuen.

Department of Education and Science (DES). 1975. *Curricula Differences for Boys and Girls in Mixed and Single-Sex Schools.* London: Her Majesty's Stationery Office (Education Survey 21).

Downing, John A. 1973. *Comparative Reading: Cross National Studies of Behavior and Processes in Reading and Writing.* New York: Macmillan.

Doyle, Sister Margaret Marie. 1932. *The Curriculum of the Catholic Woman's College.* Michigan: The College Press.

Draper, Andrew S. 1909. *American Education.* Boston: Houghton Mifflin.

Dujardin, Richard C. 1983. Gelineau Unveils School Merger, Stuns Teachers. *The Providence Journal,* October 14, 1, 16.

Duncan, Otis Dudley, David L. Featherman, & Beverly Duncan. 1972. *Socioeconomic Background and Achievement.* New York: Academic Press.

Dupuis, Adrian M. & Robert C. Craig. 1963. *American Education: Its Origins and Issues.* Milwaukee: The Bruce Doubleday Company.

Durkheim, Emile. 1965. *On the Division of Labor in Society.* Toronto: Macmillan. (Originally published in 1933.)

Dwyer, C. A. Fall 1973. Sex Differences in Reading: An Evaluation and a Critique of Current Methods. *Review of Educational Research* 43, 455–467.

Eagly, Alice H. 1978. Sex Differences in Influenceability. *Psychological Bulletin* 85, 85–116.

Educational Amendments of 1972. 1972. Section 901. *Laws of 92 U.S. Congress,* Second Session.

Ekstrom, Ruth B., Margaret E. Goertz, & Donald E. Rock. 1986. Student Achievement. In Jane Hannaway & Marlaine E. Lockheed (eds.), *The Contributions of the Social Sciences to Educational Policy and Practice: 1965–1985.* Berkeley: McCutchan, 71–97.

Entwisle, Doris R. & Leslie A. Hayduk. 1982. *Early Schooling: Cognitive and Affective Outcomes.* Baltimore: Johns Hopkins University Press.

Epstein, Joyce L. 1987. Toward a Theory of Family–School Connections: Teacher Practices and Parent Involvement Across the School Years. In D. Hurrelmann, F. Kaufmann, & F. Losel (eds.), *Social Intervention: Potential and Constraints.* New York: de Gruyta Press.

Feldblum, Chai R., Nancy Fredman Krent, & Virginia G. Watkin. 1986. Legal Challenges to All-Female Organizations. *Harvard Civil Rights—Civil Liberties Law Review* 21, 171–225.

Finn, Chester. 1983. The Futile Quest for No-Fault Excellence in Education. *Education Week,* November 23, 3, 19, 24.

Finn, Jeremy D. 1980. Sex Differences in Educational Outcomes. *Sex Roles* 6, 9–26.

Finn, Jeremy D., Loretta Dulberg, & Janet Reis. 1979. Sex Differences in Educational Attainment: A Cross-national Perspective. *Harvard Educational Review* 49, 477–503.

Finn, Jeremy D., Janet Reis, & Loretta Dulberg. 1980. Sex Differences in Educational Attainment: The Process. *Comparative Education Review* 24, 233–252.

Fishel, Andrew & Janice Pottker. 1977a. *National Politics and Sex Discrimination in Education*. Lexington, MA: D. C. Heath.

Fishel, Andrew & Janice Pottker. 1977b. Sex Bias in Secondary Schools: The Impact of Title IX. In Janice Pottker & Andrew Fishel (eds.), *Sex Bias in the Schools*. Teaneck, NJ: Fairleigh Dickenson University Press, 92–104.

Fisher, Rabbi Joseph. July 15, 1986. Personal Correspondence. National Society for Hebrew Day Schools, 160 Broadway, New York.

Fisher, Rabbi Joseph. October 14, 1988. Personal Correspondence. National Society for Hebrew Day Schools, 160 Broadway, New York.

Fleming, Jacquelin. 1984. *Blacks in College: A Comparative Study of Students' Success in Black and in White Institutions*. San Francisco: Jossey-Bass.

Fox, Lynn H. 1977. The Effects of Sex Role Socialization on Mathematics Participation and Achievement. In L. H. Fox, E. Fennema, & J. Sherman (eds.). *Women and Mathematics: Research Perspectives for Change*. Washington, DC: National Institute of Education.

Fuller, Bruce. 1986. Defining School Quality. In Jane Hannaway & Marlaine E. Lockheed (eds.), *The Contributions of the Social Sciences to Educational Policy and Practice: 1965–1985*. Berkeley: McCutchan, 33–69.

Gappa, Judith M. & Barbara S. Uehling. 1979. *Women in Academe: Steps to Greater Equality*. Washington, DC: The American Association for Higher Education.

Gardner, John W. 1961. *Excellence: Can We Be Equal and Excellent Too?* New York: Harper & Brothers.

Ginzberg, Lori D. 1987. The "Joint Education of the Sexes": Oberlin's Original Vision. In Carol Lasser (ed.), *Educating Men and Women Together: Coeducation in a Changing World*. Urbana, IL: University of Illinois Press.

Goldberger, Arthur S. & Glen G. Cain. 1982. The Causal Analysis of Cognitive Outcomes in the Coleman, Hoffer and Kilgore Report. *Sociology of Education* 55, 103–122.

Good, Thomas L. & M. J. Findley. 1982. *Sex Role Expectations and Achievement*. Unpublished manuscript.

Goodlad, John I. 1984. *A Place Called School*. New York: McGraw-Hill.

Gordon, Chad. 1972. *Looking Ahead: Self-Conceptions, Race and Family as Determinants of Adolescent Orientation to Achievement*. Washington, DC: The American Sociology Association.

Graham, Patricia A. 1978. Expansion and Exclusion: A History of Women in American Higher Education. *Signs: Journal of Women in Culture and Society* 3, 759–773.

Grant, W. Vance & Leo J. Eiden. 1981. *Digest of Education Statistics*. Washington, DC: National Center for Education Statistics, U.S. Government Printing Office.

Grant, W. Vance & C. George Lind. 1973. *Digest of Education Statistics*. Washington, DC: National Center for Education Statistics, U.S. Government Printing Office.

Grant, W. Vance & Thomas D. Snyder. 1983. *Digest of Education Statistics.* Washington, DC: National Center for Education Statistics, U.S. Government Printing Office.

Greeley, Andrew M. 1982. *Catholic High Schools and Minority Students.* New Brunswick, NJ: Transaction Books.

Green, Max. 1984. Thinking Realistically About Integration. *New Perspectives* (U.S. Commission on Civil Rights) 16.

Greenough, Richard. 1970. Coeducation as a World Trend. *School and Society,* January, 31–32.

Hacker, Andrew. 1983. *U/S: A Statistical Portrait of the American People.* New York: Viking Press.

Hale, Beatrice Forbes-Robertson. 1929. A Debate on Coeducation. *Minnesota Chats* 11, 7–9.

Hall, Roberta R. & Bernice R. Sandler. 1982. *The Classroom Climate: A Chilly One for Women.* Project on the Status and Education of Women, Association of American Colleges, Washington, DC.

Halsey, Albert Henry. 1972. *Trends in British Society Since 1900: A Guide to the Changing Social Structure of Britain.* London: Macmillan.

Hamilton, Marlene A. 1985. Performance Levels in Science and Other Subjects for Jamaican Adolescents Attending Single-Sex and Co-Educational High Schools. *Science Education* 69, 535–547.

Hamilton, Stephen F. 1986. Raising Standards and Reducing Dropout Rates. In Gary Natriello (ed.), *School Dropouts: Patterns and Policies.* New York: Teachers College Press, 148–167.

Hanna, Gila & Erika Kuendiger. 1986. Differences in Mathematical Achievement Levels and Attitudes for Girls and Boys in Twenty Countries. Paper presented at the annual meeting of the American Educational Research Association, San Francisco.

Hannon, Damian et al. 1983. *Schooling and Sex Roles: Sex Differences in Subject Provision and Student Choice in Irish Post Primary Schools.* Dublin: The Economic and Social Research Institute.

Hansot, Elizabeth and David Tyack. 1988. Gender in American Public Schools: Thinking Institutionally. *Signs: Journal of Women in Culture and Society* 13, 741–760.

Hanushek, Erik. 1986. The Economics of Schooling: Production and Efficiency in Public Schools. *Journal of Economic Literature* 24, 1141–1177.

Harnquist, Kjell. 1977. Enduring Effects of Schooling—A Neglected Area in Educational Research. *Educational Researcher* 6, 5–11.

Harvard Education Letter. February 1985. 1, 1–3.

Hawtrey, Mabel. 1896. *The Coeducation of the Sexes.* London: Kegan Paul, Trench, Trubner & Co.

Heyneman, Stephen P. & D. T. Jamison. 1980. Student Learning in Uganda: Textbook Availability and Other Factors. *Comparative Education Review* 23, 202–220.

Heyneman, Stephen P. & William A. Loxley. 1983. The Effect of Primary-School Quality on Academic Achievement Across Twenty-Nine High- and

Low-Income Countries. *American Journal of Sociology* 88, 1162–1194.

Heynes, Barbara. 1978. *Summer Learning and the Effects of Schooling*. New York: Academic Press.

Heynes, Barbara. 1982. The Influence of Parents' Work on Children's School Achievement. In S. Kamerman (ed.), *Families That Work: Children in a Changing World*. Washington, DC: National Academy Press, 229–267.

Heynes, Barbara & Thomas L. Hilton. 1982. The Cognitive Tests for High School and Beyond: An Assessment. *Sociology of Education* 55, 89–102.

Hoffer, Thomas, Andrew M. Greeley, & James S. Coleman. 1985. Achievement Growth in Public and Catholic Schools. *Sociology of Education* 58, 74–97.

Hollingshead, August B. 1949. *Elmtown's Youth*. New York: Wiley.

Hughes, Jean O'Gorman & Bernice Sandler. 1988. *Peer Harassment, Hassles for Women on Campus*. Washington, DC: Project on the Status and Education of Women, Association of American Colleges.

Husen, Torsten (ed.). 1967. *International Study of Achievement in Mathematics*, Vols. I & II. New York: John Wiley.

Husen, Torsten. 1974. Implications of the IEA Findings for the Philosophy of Comprehensive Schooling. In Alan C. Purves & Daniel V. Lavine (eds.), *Educational Policy and International Assessment*. Berkeley: McCutchan, 117–143.

Hyde, Simeon Jr. 1971. The Case for Co-education. *The Independent School Bulletin* 31, 20–24.

Hyman, Herbert H., Charles R. Wright, & John S. Reed. 1975. *The Enduring Effects of Education*. Chicago: University of Chicago Press.

Iglitzin, Lynne B. & Ruth Ross. 1976. *Women in the World: A Comparative Study*. Santa Barbara, CA: American Bibliographical Center–Clio Press.

Ingalls, Zoe. 1984. Women's Colleges Show Renewed Vigor After Long, Painful Self-Examination. *Chronicle of Higher Education* 29, September 12, 1, 18, 19.

Ingalls, Zoe. 1985. Alumnae Give High Marks to Women's College Survey. *Chronicle of Higher Education*, 30, March 27, 16.

Jamison, D. & Marlaine E. Lockheed. 1987. Participation in Schooling: Determinants and Learning Outcomes in Nepal. *Economic Development and Cultural Change* 35, 279–306.

Jencks, Christopher. 1985. How Much Do High School Students Learn? *Sociology of Education* 58, 128–135.

Jencks, Christopher & David Riesman. 1968. *The Academic Revolution*. New York: Doubleday.

Jimenez, Emmanuel & Marlaine E. Lockheed. 1989. The Relative Effectiveness of Single-Sex and Coeducational Schools in Thailand. Washington, DC: The World Bank.

Johnson, Dale D. 1973. Sex Differences in Reading Across Cultures. *Reading Research Quarterly* 9(1), 67–86.

Jones, J. Charles, Jack Shallcrass, & Cathy C. Dennis. 1972. Coeducation and Adolescent Values. *Journal of Educational Psychology* 63, 334–341.

Jones, James M. 1972. *Prejudice and Racism*. Reading, MA: Addison-Wesley.

Jones, Jennifer, Noelene Kyle, & Jan Black. 1987. The Tidy Classroom: An Assessment of the Change from Single-Sex Schooling to Coeducation in New South Wales. *Australian Journal of Education* 31, 284–302.

Jones, Marshall B. & David G. Thompson. 1981. Classroom Misconduct and Integration by Sex. *Journal of Child Psychology and Psychiatry and Allied Disciplines* 22(4), 401–409.

Kahl, J. 1953. Educational and Occupational Aspirations of "Common Man" Boys. *Harvard Educational Review* 23, 186–203.

Kandel, Denise B. & Gerald S. Lesser. 1969. Parental and Peer Influences on Educational Plans of Adolescents. *American Sociological Review* 34, 212–223.

Kelly, Alison. 1978. *Girls and Science: An International Study of Sex Differences in School Science Achievement.* Stockholm: Almquist & Wiksell International.

Kerber, Linda K. 1987. Nothing Useless or Absurd or Fantastical: The Education of Women in the Early Republic. In C. Lasser (ed.), *Educating Men and Women Together.* Urbana, IL: University of Illinois Press, 37–48.

Kilgore, Sally B. 1983. Statistical Evidence, Selectivity Effects and Program Placement: Response to Alexander and Pallas. *Sociology of Education* 56, 182–186.

Kilgore, Sally B. 1984. Schooling Effects: Reply to Alexander and Pallas. *Sociology of Education* 57, 59–61.

Klainin, Suneee & Peter Fensham. 1986. Gender Differences in Science Learning. Paper presented at the annual meeting of the American Educational Research Association, San Francisco.

Klein, Susan S. 1985. *Handbook for Achieving Sex Equity Through Education.* Baltimore: Johns Hopkins University Press.

Kolesnik, Walter B. 1969. *Co-education: Sex Differences and the Schools.* New York: Vantage Press.

Kunkel, John K. & Richard H. Nagasawa. 1973. A Behavioral Model of Man: Propositions and Implications. *American Sociological Review* 38, 530–543.

Larkin, Ralph W. 1979. *Suburban Youth in Cultural Crisis.* New York: Oxford University Press.

Lee, Valerie E. & Anthony S. Bryk. 1986. Effects of Single-sex Secondary Schools on Student Achievement and Attitudes. *Journal of Educational Psychology* 78, 381–395.

Lee, Valerie E. & Marlaine E. Lockheed. 1989. The Effects of Single-Sex Schooling on Student Achievement and Attitudes in Nigeria. Paper presented at the annual meeting of the American Educational Research Association, San Francisco.

Lee, Valerie E. & Helen M. Marks. 1989. Sustained Effects of the Single-Sex Secondary School Experience on Attitudes, Behaviors, and Values in College. Paper presented at the annual meeting of the American Educational Research Association, San Francisco.

Linn, Robert L., George F. Madaus, & Joseph J. Pedulla. 1982. Minimum Competency Testing: Cautions on the State of the Art. *American Journal of Education* 91, 1–35.

Lockheed, Marlaine E. 1976. Legislation Against Sex Discrimination: Implications for Research. Paper presented at the annual meeting of the American Educational Research Association, San Francisco.

Lockheed, Marlaine E. 1982. Sex Equity in Classroom Interaction Research: An Analysis of Behavior Chains. Paper presented at the annual meeting of the American Educational Research Association, New York.

Lockheed, Marlaine E. 1985. *Gender Segregation: The Issue of the Eighties.* Address given at the annual meeting of the American Educational Research Association, Chicago.

Lockheed, Marlaine E. 1985. Sex and Social Influence: A Meta-analysis Guided by Theory. In Joseph Berger & Morris Zelditch, Jr. (eds.), *Status, Rewards, and Influence.* San Francisco: Jossey-Bass, 406–427.

Lockheed, Marlaine E. & Katherine P. Hall. 1976. Conceptualizing Sex as a Status Characteristic: Applications to Leadership Training Strategies. *Journal of Social Issues* 32, 111–124.

Lockheed, Marlaine E. & Abigail M. Harris. 1984. Cross-Sex Collaborative Learning in Elementary Classrooms. *American Educational Research Journal* 21, 275–294.

Lockheed, Marlaine E., Abigail M. Harris, & William P. Nemceff. 1983. Sex and Social Influence: Does Sex Function as a Status Characteristic in Mixed-Sex Groups in Children? *Journal of Educational Psychology* 75, 877–888.

Lockheed, Marlaine E. & Susan S. Klein. 1985. Sex Equity in Classroom Organization and Climate. In Susan S. Klein (ed.), *Handbook for Achieving Sex Equity Through Education.* Baltimore: Johns Hopkins University Press, 189–217.

Lockheed, Marlaine E. & Andre Komenan. 1988. *School Effects on Student Achievement in Africa: The Case of Nigeria and Swaziland.* Discussion paper, Population and Human Resource Series. Washington, DC: The World Bank.

Lynd, Robert S. & Helen M. Lynd. 1929. *Middletown: A Study of American Culture.* New York: Harcourt, Brace and World.

MacDonald, C. T. 1980. An Experiment in Mathematics Education at the College Level. In Lynn H. Fox, Linda Brody, & Dianne Tobin (eds.), *Women and the Mathematical Mystique.* Baltimore: Johns Hopkins University Press.

Marrou, Henri I. 1956. *A History of Education in Antiquity.* Translated by George Lamb. New York: Sheed and Ward.

Mary Janet, Sister. 1949. *Catholic Secondary Education: A National Survey.* Washington, DC: National Catholic Welfare Conference.

McClendon, McKee J. 1974. Interracial Contact and the Reduction of Prejudice. *Sociological Forces* 4, 47–65.

McDill, Edward L., Edmund D. Meyers, Jr., & Leo C. Rigsby. 1967. Institutional Effects on the Academic Behavior of High School Students. *Sociology of Education* 40, 181–199.

McDill, Edward L., Gary Natriello, & Aaron M. Pallas. 1985. Raising Standards and Retaining Students: The Impact of the Reform Recommendations on Potential Dropouts. *Review of Educational Research* 55, 415–433.

McDill, Edward L. & Leo C. Rigsby. 1973. *The Academic Impact of Educational Climates*. Baltimore: Johns Hopkins University Press.

McGrath, Noreen. 1979. Coeducation May Place Women at a Disadvantage, Study Finds. *Chronicle of Higher Education* January, 8, 20.

McGrath, Patricia L. 1976. *The Unfinished Assignment: Equal Education for Women*. Washington, DC: Worldwatch Institute.

McPartland, James M. & Edward L. McDill. 1982. Control and Differentiation in the Structure of American Education. *Sociology of Education* 55, 77–88.

Meeker, B. F. & P. A. Weitzel-O'Neill. 1977. Sex Roles and Interpersonal Behavior in Task-Oriented Groups. *American Sociological Review* 42, 91–105.

Miller, Norman & Marilynn B. Brewer (eds.). 1984. *Groups in Contact: The Psychology of Desegregation*. New York: Academic Press.

Milne, Ann N., David E. Myers, Alan Ginsburg, & Alvin S. Rosenthal. 1986. Single Parents, Working Mothers, and the Educational Achievement of Elementary School Children. *Sociology of Education* 59, 125–139.

Mosteller, Frederick & Daniel P. Moynihan. 1972. *On Equality of Educational Opportunity*. New York: Random House.

Mulligan, Hugh A. 1985. America's Alma Mater, Boston Latin, Turns 350. *The Providence Sunday Journal*, April 7, A–17.

Nash, S. C. 1975. The Relationship Among Sex-Role Stereotyping, Sex-Role Preference and the Sex Difference in Spatial Visualization. *Sex Roles*, 1, 15–32.

National Education Association. 1893. *Report of the Committee on Secondary School Studies*. Washington, DC: United States Government Printing Office.

National Institute of Education. 1984. *School Desegregation and Black Achievement*. Washington, DC: Office of Education Policy and Organization.

Nehrt, Roy C. 1981. *Private Schools in American Education*. Washington, DC: National Center for Education Statistics.

Newcomer, M. 1959. *A Century of Higher Education for American Women*. New York: Harper & Brothers.

Oakes, Jeannie. 1985. *Keeping Track: How Schools Structure Inequality*. New Haven, CT: Yale University Press.

Oates, Mary J. & Susan Williamson. 1978. Women's Colleges and Women Achievers. *Signs: Journal of Women in Culture and Society* 3, 795–806.

Oates, Mary J. & Susan Williamson. 1980. Comment on Tidball's "Women's Colleges and Women Achievers Revisited." *Signs: Journal of Women in Culture and Society* 6, 342–345.

Oliver, Laurel W. 1975. Counseling Implications of Recent Research on Women. *Personnel and Guidance Journal* 53, 430–437.

Orfield, Gary. 1976. Will Separate Be More Equal? *Integrated Education*, January/February, 3–5.

Page, Ellis B. & Gary M. Grandon. 1979. Family Configuration and Mental

Ability: Two Theories Contrasted with U.S. Data. *American Educational Research Journal* 16, 257–273.

Palardy, J. Michael. 1969. What Teachers Believe—What Children Achieve. *Elementary School Journal* 69, 370–374.

Palmieri, Patricia A. 1987. From Republican Motherhood to Race Suicide: Arguments on the Higher Education of Women in the United States, 1820–1920. In Carol Lasser (ed.), *Educating Men and Women Together.* Urbana, IL: University of Illinois Press, 49–66.

Parry, J. & N. Parry. 1974. The Teachers and Professionalism: The Failure of an Occupational Strategy. In M. Flude & J. Ahier (eds.), *Educability, Schools and Ideology.* London: Croom-Helm.

Pettigrew, Thomas F. 1971. *Racially Separate or Together.* New York: McGraw-Hill.

Pietrofesa, John J. and N. K. Schlossberg. 1977. Counselor Bias and the Female Occupational Rule. In Janice M. Pottker and Andrew Fishel (eds.), *Sex Bias in the Schools.* Teaneck, NJ: Fairleigh Dickenson University Press, 221–229.

Plessy v. Ferguson. 1896. 163 U.S. 537.

Postlethwaite, T. Neville. 1988. Cross National Convergence of Concepts and Measurement of Educational Achievement. Paper presented at the annual meeting of the American Educational Research Association, New Orleans.

Powell, Arthur G., Eleanor Farrar, & David K. Cohen. 1985. *The Shopping Mall High School.* Boston: Houghton Mifflin.

Powell, Barbara S. & Arthur G. Powell. 1983. For Girls, Schools of Their Own. *Independent School* 43, 55–58.

Power, Edward J. 1958. *A History of Catholic Higher Education in the United States.* Milwaukee, WI: The Bruce Publishing Co.

Power, Edward J. 1970. *Main Currents in the History of Education.* New York: McGraw-Hill.

Psacharopoulos, G. & A. M. Arriagada. 1987. School Participation, Grade Attainment and Literacy in Brazil: A 1980 Census Analysis. Washington, DC: The World Bank, Education and Training Department.

Pugh, M. D. & Ralph Wahrman. 1983. Neutralizing Sexism in Mixed-Sex Groups: Do Women Have To Be Better Than Men? *American Journal of Sociology* 88, 746–762.

Raspberry, William. 1987. Plan for Black Education is Bold Step for Milwaukee. *The Providence Journal,* November 21.

Rawls, John. 1971. *A Theory of Justice.* Cambridge, MA: Belknap Press of Harvard University Press.

Read, F. 1975. Judicial Evolution of the Law of School Integration Since *Brown v. Board of Education. Law and Contemporary Problems* 39, 7–49.

Remmers, Hermann H. & D. H. Radler. 1957. *The American Teenager.* Indianapolis: Bobbs-Merrill.

Rich, Adrienne. 1979. Taking Women Students Seriously. In *On Lies, Secrets and Silence.* New York: W. W. Norton, Co.

Rich, D. 1985. *The Forgotten Factor in School Success: The Family*. Washington, DC: Home and School Institute.

Riordan, Cornelius. 1978. Equal-Status Interracial Contact: A Review and Revision of the Concept. *International Journal of Intercultural Relations* 2, 161–185.

Riordan, Cornelius. 1983. Sex as a Status Characteristic. *Social Psychology Quarterly* 46, 261–267.

Riordan, Cornelius. 1985. Public and Catholic Schooling: The Effects of Gender Context Policy. *American Journal of Education* 93, 518–540.

Riordan, Cornelius. 1987. Gender Context and Educational Achievement. Paper read at the annual meeting of the American Educational Research Association, New Orleans.

Rosenbaum, James E. 1980. Social Implications of Educational Grouping. In David C. Berliner (ed.), *Review of Research in Education*, Vol. 8. Washington, DC: American Educational Research Association, 361–401.

Rosenberg, Morris. 1965. *Society and the Adolescent Self-Image*. Princeton, NJ: Princeton University Press.

Rosenberg, Morris & Roberta G. Simmons. 1972. *Black and White Self-Esteem: The Urban School Child*. Washington, DC: American Sociological Association.

Rosenthal, Robert & Lenore Jacobson. 1968. *Pygmalion in the Classroom*. New York: Holt, Rinehart & Winston.

Rossell, Christine H. & Willis D. Hawley. 1983. *The Consequences of School Desegregation*. Philadelphia: Temple University Press.

Sadler, Michael E. 1903. An Introduction. In Alice Woods (ed.), *Coeducation*. London: Longmans, Green.

St. John, Nancy H. 1975. *School Desegregation: Outcomes for Children*. New York: John Wiley.

Sarah, Elizabeth, Marion Scott, & Dale Spender. 1980. The Education of Feminists: The Case for Single-Sex Schools. In Dale Spender & Elizabeth Sarah (eds.), *Learning to Lose*. London: Women's Press, 55–66.

Schneider, Frank W. & Larry M. Coutts. 1982. The High School Environment: A Comparison of Co-educational and Single Sex Schools. *Journal of Educational Psychology* 74, 898–906.

Schwager, Sally. 1987. Educating Women in America. *Signs: Journal of Women in Culture and Society* 12, 333–372.

Sedlak, Michael W., Christopher W. Wheeler, Diana C. Pullin, & Philip A. Cusik. 1986. *Selling Students Short: Classroom, Bargains and Academic Reform in the American High School*. New York: Teachers College Press.

Seewald, Andrea M., Gaea Leinhart, & Mary Engel. 1977. *Learning What's Taught: Sex Differences in Instruction*. Pittsburgh: University of Pittsburgh, Learning Research and Development Center.

Seller, Maxine S. 1983. Dr. Clarke Vs. The "Ladies": Coeducation and Women's Roles in the 1870s. Paper presented at the annual meeting of the American Educational Research Association,

Sexton, Patricia. 1969. *The Feminized Male: Classrooms, White Collar and the Decline of Manliness.* New York: Random House.

Sexton, Patricia. 1976. *Women in Education.* Indiana: Phi Delta Kappa Educational Foundation.

Seybolt, Robert F. 1925. Source Studies in American Colonial Education: The Private School. *University of Illinois Bulletin* 23, entire issue.

Shafer, Susanne. 1976. The Socialization of Girls in Secondary Schools of England and the Two Germanies. *International Review of Education* 22, 5–25.

Sharp, Marcia. 1979. Women's Colleges: Equity and Optimum. *College Board Review,* 3, 18–21.

Shaw, Jennifer. 1976. Finishing School: Some Implications of Sex-Segregated Education. In D. L. Barker & Sheila Allen (eds.), *Sexual Division and Society: Process and Change.* London: Tavistock Publications, 133–149.

Shaw, Jennifer. 1980. Education and the Individual: Schooling for Girls or Mixed Schooling—A Mixed Blessing? In Rosemary Deem (ed.), *Schooling for Women's Work.* London: Routledge & Kegan Paul, 66–75.

Shaw, Jennifer. 1984. The Politics of Single Sex Schools. In Rosemary Deem (ed.), *Co-Education Reconsidered.* Milton Keynes, England: Open University Press, 21–35.

Simmons, J. & L. Alexander. 1978. The Determinants of School Achievement in Developing Countries: A Review of the Research. *Economic Development and Cultural Change* 26, 341–357.

Simpson, George E. & J. Milton Yinger. 1985. *Racial and Cultural Minorities: An Analysis of Prejudice and Discrimination.* New York: Plenum.

Solomon, Barbara Miller. 1985. *In The Company of Educated Women.* New Haven: Yale University Press.

Sowell, Thomas. 1976. Patterns of Black Excellence. *The Public Interest* 43, 26–58.

Spaeth, Joe L. 1976. Cognitive Complexity: A Dimension Underlying the Socioeconomic Achievement Process. In William H. Sewell, Robert M. Hauser, & David L. Featherman (eds.), *Schooling and Achievement in American Society.* New York: Academic Press, 103–131.

Spender, Dale. 1982. *Invisible Women: The Schooling Scandal.* London: Writers and Readers Publishing Cooperative.

Stedman, L. C. & M. S. Smith. 1983. Recent Reform Proposals for American Education. *Contemporary Education Review* 2, 85–104.

Steelman, Lala C. & James A. Mercy. 1980. Unconfounding the Confluence Model: A Test of Sibship Size and Birth-Order Effects on Intelligence. *American Sociological Review* 45, 571–582.

Stein, A. H. & J. S. Smithells. 1969. Age and Sex Differences in Children's Sex-Role Standard About Achievement. *Developmental Psychology* 1, 252–259.

Stephan, Walter G. & Joe R. Feagin (eds.). 1980. *School Desegregation: Past, Present & Future.* New York: Plenum.

Sterling, Richard W. & William C. Scott. 1985. *The Republic: A New Translation.* New York: Norton.

Stimpson, Catharine R. 1987. New Consciousness, Old Institutions, and the Need for Reconciliation. In Carol Lasser (ed.), *Educating Men and Women Together*. Urbana, IL: University of Illinois Press, 155–164.

Stock, Phyllis. 1978. *Better Than Rubies: A History of Women's Education*. New York: G. P. Putnam's Sons.

Stoecker, Judith L. & Ernest Pascarella. 1988. Institutional Gender and the Early Educational and Economic Attainments of Women. Paper read at the annual meeting of the American Educational Research Association, New Orleans.

Tajfel, Henri. 1969. Cognitive Aspects of Prejudice. *Journal of Social Issues 25*, 79–97.

Terman, Lewis M. & Catherine C. Miles. 1936. *Sex and Personality*. New York: McGraw-Hill.

Thomas, Arthur H. & Norman R. Stewart. 1971. Counselor Response to Female Clients with Deviate and Conforming Career Goals. *Journal of Counseling Psychology 18*, 352–357.

Thomas, M. Carey. 1900. Education of Women. In Nicholas M. Butler (ed.), *Education in the United States*. New York: American Book Company.

Tidball, M. Elizabeth. 1973. Perspective on Academic Women and Affirmative Action. *Educational Record 54*, 130–135.

Tidball, M. Elizabeth. 1980. Women's Colleges and Women Achievers Revisted. *Signs: Journal of Women in Culture and Society*, 504–517.

Tomlinson, T. W. 1988. Class Size and Public Policy: Politics and Panaceas. Washington, DC: Office of Educational Research and Improvement, U.S. Department of Education.

Trickett, Edison J., Penelope K. Trickett, Julie J. Castro, & Paul Schaffner. 1982. The Independent School Experience: Aspects of the Normative Environments of Single-Sex and Coed Secondary Schools. *Journal of Educational Psychology 74*, 374–381.

Trow, Martin. 1961. The Second Transformation of American Secondary Education. *The International Journal of Comparative Sociology 2*, 144–166.

Twentieth Century Fund. 1983. *Making The Grade: Report of the Twentieth Century Task Force on Federal Elementary and Secondary Education Policy*. New York: Twentieth Century Fund.

Tyack, David & Elizabeth Hansot. 1988. Silence and Policy Talk: Historical Puzzles About Gender and Education. *Educational Researcher 17*, 33–41.

Uhlig, Mark A. 1987. Learning Style of Minorities to be Studied. *The New York Times*, November 21, 29.

U.S. Commissioner of Education. 1901. *Report for 1901*. Washington, DC: U.S. Government Printing Office.

Vockell, Edward L. & Susan Lobonc. 1981. Sex-Role Stereotyping by High School Females in Science. *Journal of Research in Science Teaching 18*, 209–219.

Walberg, Herbert J. 1985. Educational Strategies That Work. *New Perspectives* (U.S. Commission on Civil Rights) 17, Winter, 23–26.

Walberg, Herbert J. & Kevin Marjoribanks. 1976. Family Environment and Cognitive Development: Twelve Analytic Models. *Review of Educational Research* 46, 527–551.

Webb, Noreen M. 1982. Sex Differences in Interaction and Achievement in Cooperative Small Groups. Paper presented at the Second International Conference on Cooperation in Education, Provo, Utah.

Webb, Rodman B. & Robert R. Sherman. 1989. *Schooling and Society* (2nd ed.). New York: Macmillan.

Whelan, James F. 1952. *Catholic Colleges of the United States of America in the Middle of the Twentieth Century.* New Orleans, LA: Loyola University Bookstore.

Williams, John Edwin, S. M. Bennett, & D. L. Best. 1975. Awareness and Expression of Sex Stereotypes in Young Children. *Developmental Psychology* 11, 635–642.

Willis, Paul. 1977. *Learning to Labor.* Hampshire, England: Gower Publishing House, Ltd.

Willms, J. Douglas. 1985. Catholic School Effects on Academic Achievement: New Evidence from the High School and Beyond Follow-Up Study. *Sociology of Education* 58, 98–114.

Wilson, George. 1983. Viewpoint—The Right Decision for Central High. *Philadelphia Inquirer,* September 9, A13.

Winchel, Ronald, Diane Fenner, & Philip Shaver. 1974. Impact of Co-education on Fear of Success Imagery Expressed by Male and Female High School Students. *Journal of Educational Psychology* 66, 726–730.

Wolfle, Lee M. 1980. The Enduring Effects of Education on Verbal Skills. *Sociology of Education* 53, 104–114.

Woods, M. B. 1972. The Unsupervised Child of the Working Mother. *Developmental Psychology* 6, 14–25.

Zajonc, Robert B. 1976. Family Configuration and Intelligence. *Science* 192, 227–336.

Index

Page numbers followed by *n* indicate footnotes or sourcenotes.

About the Author

Cornelius Riordan is a sociologist and educational researcher. His research interests are the study of school effects and the organization of schools. He received his M.A. from Clark University and his Ph.D. from Syracuse University, and was a postdoctoral fellow at Johns Hopkins University. Dr. Riordan is Associate Professor of Sociology at Providence College. He teaches sociology of education in the departments of both sociology and education.